Also by Stephen Goode
The New Congress

The Controversial Court

Supreme
Court
Influences on American Life

by Stephen Goode

JULIAN MESSNER
NEW YORK

Published by Julian Messner, a Simon & Schuster
Division of Gulf & Western Corporation.
Simon & Schuster Building,
1230 Avenue of the Americas,
New York, New York 10020.
JULIAN MESSNER and colophon are trademarks of
Simon & Schuster.

Manufactured in the United States of America
Second printing, 1982
Design by Irving Perkins Associates

Library of Congress Cataloging in Publication Data

Goode, Stephen.
    The controversial court.

    Bibliography: p. 185
    Includes index.
    1. United States.   Supreme Court—Juvenile
literature.   2. United States—Constitutional
law—Cases—Juvenile literature.   I. Title.
KF8742.Z9G66   347.73′26   82-3498
                    347.30735   AACR2

ISBN:0-671-43656-2

This book is dedicated
to the memory of my father,
Ersel Goode, 1903–1980

Contents

	Introduction	9
CHAPTER ONE	The Power of the Supreme Court	13
PART ONE	**The Warren Court: An Activist Court in Action**	**25**
CHAPTER TWO	*Brown* v. *Board of Education*	27
CHAPTER THREE	The Reaction to *Brown*	44
CHAPTER FOUR	One Person, One Vote	58
CHAPTER FIVE	The Warren Court and the Rights of the Accused	71
CHAPTER SIX	The Warren Court and Religion	85
CHAPTER SEVEN	Postscript on the Warren Court	99
PART TWO	**The Burger Court: Transition to Judicial Conservatism**	**107**
CHAPTER EIGHT	The Crisis of Transition	109
CHAPTER NINE	The Burger Court and the Rights of Criminals	129
CHAPTER TEN	Reapportionment and Race Relations	145
CHAPTER ELEVEN	Four Important Cases	163

CHAPTER TWELVE The Character of the
                Burger Court   177

                Suggested Further Reading   185

                Index   187

Introduction

Hardly any question arises in the United States that is not resolved sooner or later into a judicial question—from *Democracy in America* (1835) by Alexis de Tocqueville.

This is a book about the Supreme Court during the past thirty years. In that time, the Court has been led by two chief justices, Earl Warren (1953–1969) and Warren Burger (1969–   ). Twenty-one men and one woman have served in the eight positions of associate justice, several with great distinction. By tradition, however, the Supreme Court is identified by the name of the chief justice who sits at its head.

The Warren Court and the Burger Court contrast vividly. Chief Justice Warren initiated what historians have called the "Warren revolution," which brought changes in race relations, voting rights, criminal law, and many other aspects of American society. The Warren Court was a liberal and an activist court, willing to take controversial stands on complex issues.

The Burger Court has been more moderate and conservative. Where the Warren Court made full use of the power and authority granted the Court by the Constitution and judicial tradition, the Burger Court has tried to play a more modest and restrained role in government. Where the Warren Court was apt to approve of immediate and sweeping changes, the Burger Court has been more cautious and prudent.

Both Courts, however, have been embroiled in controversy. The Warren Court received widespread criticism and denunciation for its decisions concerning segregation, criminals' rights, reapportionment, and school prayer. The Burger Court has been attacked for its decisions involving abortion, school busing, and the death penalty. Both Courts have been accused of "making law" rather than merely "interpreting" it and of enforcing their views on an American public unwilling to accept them.

Almost one hundred fifty years ago, the French nobleman, Alexis de Tocqueville, after a nine-month visit to the United States, noted that almost every question or problem that arose in America became "sooner or later . . . a judicial question." His observation still holds true today and helps explain why the Supreme Court has so often been at the center of political controversy during the past thirty years.

Because it is the highest court in the land and the "court of final appeal," the Supreme Court must make decisions on the deepest social, political, and moral concerns of the American people. These decisions affect the life of every citizen and help determine the course of American history. Thus the content of these decisions is important to us all. Because they are so significant, they cannot help being controversial.

De Tocqueville also noted the unusual "power" possessed by the Supreme Court in the United States. That power, he believed, was "immense" and sprang from the fact that in America the high court had the right to declare a law unconstitutional. And the power to say what the Constitution means has placed the Court at the center of the American system of government.

In the first chapter, we shall look at the Supreme Court's power and how the Court has exercised that power. We shall then turn to the major decisions of the Warren and Burger Courts, contrasting the styles and approaches of the two Courts and discussing the controversies they aroused. The story of the Warren and Burger courts tells us much about American government and how it works. It also tells us something about American society and the direction in which it is now moving.

CHAPTER ONE

The Power of the Supreme Court

> We are under a Constitution, but the Constitution is what the Supreme Court says it is—a 1907 statement by Charles Evans Hughes, three years before he was appointed to the Supreme Court.

The Supreme Court is a unique institution. Only in America, among the major democracies, does tradition grant a high court the power to overrule—and void—actions taken by the chief executive and the legislature. This power has given the Court the ability to restrict the authority of the President and Congress, change American institutions, and remold society.

The Constitution and the Supreme Court

Article III of the Constitution established the federal judiciary as a separate and equal branch of government, with "one Supreme Court" at its head. It was an unprecedented move. In England and the rest of Europe, courts had developed as part of the sovereign's "administrative household" and were therefore part of the executive. In the United States, however, the Founding Fathers wanted a judiciary that had authority of its own and that owed no allegiance to the President or Congress.

Article III likewise declared that the power of the judiciary would extend to all cases in law arising under the Constitution and federal laws, including treaties and "all cases of admiralty and maritime jurisdiction." In addition, it gave the judiciary authority over controversies between citizens of different states, between one state and another state, between a state and a citizen of another state, and between a state and the nation.

In the words of constitutional scholar R. Kent Newmyer, final jurisdiction in these areas puts the Supreme Court "at the nerve center of public power and enables it to shape the political, economic, and social issues which depend on that power." The framers of the Constitution intended the United States to be a nation in which every citizen was bound by that Constitution, but it was the federal judiciary that would have the power to say what the Constitution was.

Article III, however, did not grant the judiciary unlimited power. It required that the courts handle law on a case-by-case basis and speak only on the issues scheduled for consideration. Thus the Supreme Court, or any other federal court, can address only the problems before it and cannot turn to just any issue that might arouse its interest.

The Constitution also gave the President the power to make appointments to the Supreme Court and granted the Senate the right to consider those appointments and approve or disapprove them. The Court therefore did not control its own makeup and was subject to the will of the President and the Congress. Moreover, if justices committed bribery, treason, or other "high crimes or misdemeanors," they could be impeached by the House of Representatives and removed from office by the Senate.

Nor did the Constitution bestow on the Supreme Court any power of its own to enforce its decisions. For enforcement of its decisions, the Court must turn to the authority of the chief executive, whose duty it is to see that the laws of the land are carried out and "executed." If a President should choose to ignore the will of the Court, then the Court would be helpless to see that its wishes were obeyed.

Thus the Constitution gave the Supreme Court significant power and authority, but made that power and authority subject to limitations by the President and the legislature. What the Constitution did not say was how the Court was to exercise that power in its day-to-day proceedings. That was left to be worked out in practice.

Would the Supreme Court exert its unique power as a separate and equal branch of government or would it defer to the legislature and the executive, who were elected by the people? Just how much power did the high court possess and how should it exercise that power? These were the questions that the early leaders of the country faced, and that we are still asking today.

The Development of Judicial Review

The concept of "judicial review" is not found in the Constitution, but it has played a major role in American constitutional history. It is a controversial notion, which holds that the Supreme Court has the power to review legislation and decide on its constitutionality or unconstitutionality. In it lies a great deal of power for good or for mischief, for it grants power to the Supreme Court to have the final say on legislation passed by Congress.

The Founding Father who was the strongest defender of judicial review was Alexander Hamilton. Hamilton expressed his views on the role of the Supreme Court in *The Federalist Papers*, a series of articles written by him, James

Madison, and John Jay to explain the newly created Constitution to the people of America and to urge its approval by the thirteen colonies.

The federal judiciary, Hamilton believed, must have the authority to say what the Constitution means. The judiciary must have this authority because it is the most *disinterested* and *impartial* branch of the federal government. "Whoever attentively considers the different departments of power," Hamilton wrote, "must perceive that . . . the judiciary, from the nature of its functions, will always be the least dangerous to the political rights" guaranteed by the Constitution, "because it will be least in a capacity to annoy or injure them."

The President, he pointed out, can dispense honors and wield the military might of the nation. Congress "commands the purse" and "prescribes the rules by which the duties and rights of every citizen are to be regulated." These powers, Hamilton argued, are exceedingly great and potentially dangerous to freedom, and neither the executive nor the legislature could be trusted to interpret the Constitution impartially or to protect the laws of the land.

Both the President and Congress, he continued, would be tempted to govern by force or will and could be swayed by the passions of the moment. But the judiciary, because it was "beyond comparison the weakest of the three departments of power" and because it was separate from them, could be trusted to bring *judgment* to bear on the issues brought before it. Only the federal judiciary, with the Supreme Court at its head, would have the requisite independence and balanced reason needed to protect the Constitution from violation and misinterpretation.

Hamilton believed that "the courts were designed to be an intermediate body between the people and the legislature in order, among other things, to keep" the members of the legislature "within the limits assigned to their authority." He therefore believed that the Court had the right to review legislation and decide if it was in keeping with the principles of the Constitution: "A constitution is, in fact, and must be regarded by the judges as, a fundamental law. It therefore belongs to them to ascertain its meaning as well as the meaning of any particular act proceeding from the legislative body." If the Supreme Court judged an act of Congress to be unconstitutional, he concluded, then that act was null and void, for "no legislative act . . . contrary to the Constitution, can be valid."

Hamilton's views seem commonplace today, but in his time they were at first not widely accepted. During the first decade of its existence, the Supreme Court was weak and uncertain of the nature of its authority. So low was its prestige that many prominent Americans, including Hamilton, refused appointment to the Court and preferred a position in the President's cabinet or election to Congress.

A major change in the Court's status did not come until 1801, with the appointment of John Marshall as chief justice. Marshall, a member of a prominent Virginia family, was a firm believer in a centralized and strong federal government to check the power of the often unruly and unmanageable states. Under him, the Supreme Court first began to play a major role in government and to assume the position the Constitution designed for it.

Marshall's first great decision as chief justice was the celebrated case of *Marbury* v. *Madison*, which was handed down in February 1803. The particulars of the case need not concern us. It was Marshall's opinion that was significant and that altered the course of American constitutional history.

In his opinion, Marshall declared Section 13 of the Judiciary Act of 1789 to be unconstitutional, because, he said, in Section 13 Congress had attempted to give the Supreme Court wider jurisdiction than the Constitution permitted. This Congress could not do because the Constitution explicitly outlined the jurisdiction of the Court and Congress could not add to that jurisdiction unless the Constitution was amended.

Marbury v. *Madison* marked the first time the Court had declared a law passed by Congress to be unconstitutional. But the significance of the decision did not end there. In his commentary, Marshall went on to discuss the nature of the power of the high court, and his words have guided the history of the Court since that time.

It is "a proposition too plain to be contested," he wrote, "that the Constitution controls any legislative act repugnant to it; or, that the legislature may not alter the Constitution by an ordinary act." The Constitution is, as the document itself claims itself to be, the supreme law of the land: "If, then, the courts are to regard the Constitution, and the Constitution is superior to any ordinary Act of the Legislature, the Constitution, and not such ordinary Act, must govern the case to which they both apply."

Moreover, Marshall added, "it is emphatically the province and duty of the judicial department to say what the law is." If the Supreme Court has the power to apply the Constitution to particular cases, then it must have the right to "expound" and "interpret" that Constitution. "This," he concluded, "is of the very essence" of judicial responsibility.

Marshall presided over the Court for thirty-one years following *Marbury* v. *Madison.* Never again did his Court find an act of Congress to be unconstitutional. Nevertheless, the precedent he established remained firm. He was the first "activist" chief justice who used his position to expand the power and authority of the Court. Subsequent Supreme Courts continued to exercise the authority claimed by Marshall—echoing Hamilton's views in *The Federalist Papers*—to review legislation and pronounce on its constitutionality.

Marshall's belief in the authority of the Supreme Court aroused bitter controversy. Thomas Jefferson and his followers were horrified by what they regarded as the chief justice's blatant grab for power in *Marbury* v. *Madison.* Marshall's decision, they believed, had not resulted in judicial equality with the other branches of government, but had led to judicial supremacy—a situation in which the Supreme Court was superior in American political life, with the ability to overrule both President and Congress.

From 1803 until his death in 1825, Jefferson frequently denounced the Marshall Court. More than twenty years after *Marbury* v. *Madison,* he described Marshall's decision as "very irregular and very censurable." At about the same time, he wrote a friend that "the great object of my fear is the Federal Judiciary. That body like gravity, ever acting, with noiseless foot, and unalarming advance, gaining ground step by step, and holding what it gains, is ingulphing insidiously" the freedoms and independence enjoyed by Americans.

What aroused Jefferson's concern above all was the fear that the Supreme Court, with the powers it acquired under Marshall, would destroy the special relationship the Constitution defined between the states and the federal government. Marshall's Court, he feared, would destroy this relationship because it had given too much power to the federal judiciary and would continue to do so.

What suffered, Jefferson believed, was the very essence

of American democracy: the right of the people to determine their destiny through their own elected officials, whether at the local, state, or national levels. And in the place of this vision of democracy, he feared, was a Supreme Court that would become the protector of the wealthy, well-born, and powerful. "The Constitution," he warned his followers, "is a mere thing of wax in the hands of the judiciary which they may twist and shape into any form they please."

The Two Schools of Judicial Thought

The confrontation between Chief Justice Marshall and Thomas Jefferson helped to establish two judicial traditions in the United States, two interpretations of how the Supreme Court should use the power it possesses. On the one hand are the champions of "judicial restraint," the followers of Jefferson; on the other are the "judicial activists," the heirs of Marshall.

The champions of judicial restraint believe that the Supreme Court should be governed by the notion of *stare decisis*. *Stare decisis* is a legal expression, in Latin, which means "stand by what has already been decided." In other words, precedent should be given the authority of established law. Where earlier courts have spoken on the law, later courts should be reluctant to make changes or alterations. For the sake of continuity and stability, the past and tradition should govern judicial decisions as much as possible.

Advocates of judicial restraint also believe that the Supreme Court should be in the business of *interpreting* the law, not *making* it. The making of law, they point out, is the constitutional duty of Congress, the democratic branch of government composed of representatives elected by the people. And it is Congress, not the Supreme Court, that has the responsibility of voicing the interests and concerns of the public.

One of the most articulate advocates of judicial restraint was Justice Felix Frankfurter, who sat on the Court between 1939 and 1962. The danger of exercising "judicial power unduly," Frankfurter once wrote, was that the Court would appear to be "holding too tight a rein" on "the organs of popular government." Too tight a rein, he feared, would sap the strength of the legislature and undermine its will to innovate and experiment with new solutions to pressing problems.

The "true democratic faith," Frankfurter declared on another occasion, does not look to the Supreme Court "for the impossible task of assuring a vigorous, mature, self-protecting and tolerant democracy." Such a democracy could be established only by "the people and their representatives." The duty of the Supreme Court arose only "where the transgression of constitutional liberty" was "too plain for argument," he concluded; otherwise, the responsibility for law belonged to the Congress and the other "organs of popular government."

Judicial restraint, then, is the belief that the court should refrain from unduly challenging the right of the legislature to pass laws and express the will of the people. Only direct and clear violations of the Constitution need be declared unconstitutional. In other cases, the Court should step back and let unwise laws be changed through the political process. To do otherwise is to place the Supreme Court, the least democratic branch of the government because it is not elected by the people, in the role of a superlegislature with the power to mold social, economic, and political policy, a power that it should not have.

Advocates of judicial activism, by contrast, believe that the power of the judiciary can be used positively to achieve desirable goals. The Supreme Court, they argue, must not wear a straightjacket of its own making that prevents it from responding to change and to new judicial dilemmas. The Court must be prepared to move with the times and not adopt rigid rules that prevent it from responding creatively to the problems the future brings.

In the words of Edmond Cahn, a constitutional scholar, the work of the Supreme Court "is always more than pure and simple enforcement of the Constitution." Its work also "comprises express or tacit interpretation . . . or—in other words—a continual process of adjusting and adapting the fundamental fabric" of the Constitution to new times.

The advocates of judicial activism believe that the power of the Court is especially important when Congress or the President fails to act. Who will address a wrong or injustice, they ask, when the chief executive or the legislature ignores that wrong or injustice? When the other two branches of government are silent, only the judiciary remains to solve a problem.

In addition, the activists argue that the Supreme Court should function as what Justice Frank Murphy (who served on the Court between 1940 and 1949) called "the great pulpit." More than any other branch of the government, they point out, the Court can serve as the conscience of the nation, giving articulation to ideals that might otherwise be lost in the din of political debate and compromise.

The judicial activists believe in the practice of *stare decisis*, but they do not pay mechanical homage to it. Precedent and the judicial decisions of the past are important, but sometimes not worth the price that has to be paid for adhering to them, when that price is the continued existence of unjust or unwise laws that the Court might remedy. The Supreme Court, Justice Louis D. Brandeis wrote in 1932, should bow "to the lessons of experience and the force of better reasoning, recognizing that the process of trial and error, so fruitful in the physical sciences, is appropriate also in the judicial function."

Judicial restraint and judicial activism are two ways of handling the power possessed by the Supreme Court. The one school believes the Supreme Court should defer to Congress in the name of democracy and popular government. The other argues that the Court has a more significant role to play if it is truly to be regarded as a branch of government equal to the legislative and executive branches.

The debate between the two traditions has never been resolved, nor is resolution ever likely. The heirs of Chief Justice Marshall will continue to call for an active, dynamic Court; the followers of Jefferson will express their fears about the "unbridled" power of the federal judiciary. In the past thirty years the United States has experienced a Supreme Court that has moved from the heights of activism to the practice of moderate self-restraint, and that is the story we turn to now.

PART ONE

The Warren Court: An Activist Court in Action

The appointment of Earl Warren as Chief Justice of the United States in 1953 marked the opening of a new period in our constitutional development. In the next fifteen years the Supreme Court rewrote, with profound social consequence, major constitutional doctrines governing race relations, the administration of criminal justice, and the operation of the political process. The extent and rapidity of the changes raise grave questions concerning the proper role of the Supreme Court in our national development—questions concerning the nature and function of constitutional adjudication—Harvard Law School professor Archibald Cox in his book, *The Warren Court* (1968).

CHAPTER TWO

Brown v. Board of Education

> Our system faces no theoretical dilemma but a single continuous problem: how to apply to ever changing conditions the never changing principles of freedom—Chief Justice Earl Warren.

On May 17, 1954, the Supreme Court handed down its historic decision in the case of *Brown* v. *Board of Education*. Earl Warren had been appointed chief justice less than a year earlier, but already the character of his Court was taking shape. In a unanimous decision, the nine justices of the Supreme Court declared segregation of races in public schools to be unconstitutional.

The response to the decision was immediate and widespread. Many Americans praised the Court and argued that an end to segregation was long overdue. Others condemned the decision and accused the Court of exceeding its authority. *Brown* v. *Board of Education* signaled a new period in American judicial history. What has been called the "Warren revolution" had begun.

The Warren Court

The nine justices who handed down the *Brown* decision represented a variety of political beliefs, from moderate to

liberal. Eight had been appointed to the Court by Democratic Presidents; only one, the chief justice, had been cho-
sen by a Republican. The nine were also adherents of a
variety of judicial philosophies, from a strong advocate of
judicial restraint like Justice Frankfurter to proponents of
judicial activism like Justices Douglas and Warren.

• *Chief Justice Earl Warren.* Appointed to the Court by
President Dwight Eisenhower, Warren had a long background in Republican politics. He had served as district
attorney of Alameda County, California, where he gained a
reputation for uncovering government graft and sending
public officials to jail.

In 1942 Warren was elected governor of California and
was twice reelected. At first regarded as a conservative, he
supported the federal order to move Americans of Japanese
ancestry to special camps for the duration of World War II.
Later, however, he supported liberal causes such as improved pension and welfare benefits and a program of pre-
paid medical insurance for Californians. In 1948 he was the
Republican party's choice for Vice-President along with
presidential candidate Thomas Dewey.

• *Justice Hugo Black.* Black is regarded as one of the greatest justices in Supreme Court history. Appointed to the
Court in 1937 by President Franklin Roosevelt, he had a
long history of championing the interests of the poor and
powerless. As a young lawyer in his native Alabama, Black
defended United Mine Workers who were striking in 1908.
As a county official in Jefferson County, Alabama, between
1914 and 1918, he gained fame for his investigation of police
brutality in a local jail.

In 1926 Black ran for the Senate as the "poor man's
candidate." When Roosevelt became President, Black

wholeheartedly supported the new administration's program of liberal social and economic legislation known as the New Deal. After his appointment to the Supreme Court, he gradually became known for his strong defense of the freedoms and privileges guaranteed by the Bill of Rights.

• *Justice Stanley Reed.* A native of Kentucky, Reed was appointed to the Court in 1938 by President Roosevelt. Prior to his appointment, he had served the Roosevelt administration as solicitor general, the official responsible for arguing the government's cases before the Supreme Court, and had successfully defended several New Deal programs.

• *Justice Felix Frankfurter.* Born in Vienna, Austria, Frankfurter was reared in the tenements of New York's Lower East Side. A brilliant student at Harvard Law School, he later returned to the school to become one of its most eminent professors. He was appointed to the Supreme Court in 1939 by President Roosevelt, who was a close personal friend.

As a justice, Frankfurter was prudent and cautious, but the liberal reputation he had gained before he came to the Court stayed with him. As a younger man, he had argued minimum-wage and minimum-hour cases for the National Consumers League, defended Sacco and Vanzetti—anarchists accused and convicted of murder in a controversial case—and helped found the *New Republic*, a moderately left-wing magazine. He had also argued cases for the National Association for the Advancement of Colored People (NAACP) and was a founding member of the American Civil Liberties Union (ACLU).

• *Justice William O. Douglas.* Douglas was a native of Minnesota who grew up in the state of Washington. Regarded as a brilliant student at Columbia University Law School, he moved on after graduation to teach law at Yale. He soon gained a reputation as one of the nation's outstanding financial-law experts.

Douglas was appointed to the Court in 1939 by President Roosevelt, in whose administration he had served as head of the Securities and Exchange Commission. As a justice, Douglas was known for his strong antiestablishment views. An ardent defender of the Bill of Rights and of personal liberty, he twice faced impeachment attempts for what his opponents regarded as his outspoken radicalism and unconventional life-style.

• *Justice Robert Jackson.* Jackson rose through the ranks of the Democratic party in New York to become an able and highly regarded official in the Roosevelt administration. His strong support for the President led to his Court appointment in 1941. In 1945 and 1946 Jackson served as the chief U. S. prosecutor of Nazi war criminals at the Nuremberg trials.

• *Justice Harold Burton.* A liberal Republican, Burton had served as a reform mayor of Cleveland and as a U. S. senator from Ohio. He was appointed justice in 1945 by President Harry Truman to give balance to a Supreme Court that many believed was too heavily packed with New Deal Democrats.

• *Justice Tom Clark.* A Democrat from Texas, Clark worked in the Justice Department under Presidents Roosevelt and Truman. There he handled antitrust matters and was the civilian head of the program to move Japanese-Americans to camps during World War II. In the late 1940s he headed the Justice Department's efforts to prosecute American communists and other subversives. President Truman appointed him to the Court in 1949.

• *Justice Sherman Minton.* As a Democratic senator from

Indiana in the 1930s Minton strongly supported the New Deal. In 1941 President Roosevelt appointed him to the Seventh Circuit Court of Appeals, where he served until 1949, when President Truman elevated him to the Supreme Court. A liberal in politics, Minton nevertheless became known as one of the court's more conservative justices.

Of these nine men only two, Douglas and Black, were regarded as strong, consistently liberal justices. Chief Justice Warren's judicial views were yet to be known, and the remaining six justices were moderates—liberal on some issues, conservative on others. It was a surprise, then, when the nine voted unanimously to strike down segregation in the case of *Brown* v. *Board of Education.*

The Background of the Case

In 1866, one year after the end of the Civil War, the Thirteenth Amendment to the Constitution declared that slavery "shall not exist in the United States." Two years later, in 1868, a Fourteenth Amendment was added. Among other things, it said:

> No State shall make or enforce any law which shall abridge the privileges or immunities of citizens of the United States; nor shall any State deprive any person of life, liberty, or property, without due process of law; nor deny to any person within its jurisdiction the equal protection of the laws.

And in the following year, 1869, the Fifteenth Amendment ensured that "the right of citizens of the United States to vote shall not be denied or abridged . . . on account of race, color, or previous condition of servitude."

The three amendments were designed to root out the last vestiges of slavery and to guarantee black Americans their right to full citizenship. In 1875 Congress passed a Civil Rights Act, which was signed into law by President Ulysses S. Grant. This act recognized "the equality of all men before the law" and imposed stiff penalties for denying any citizen "full and equal enjoyment of . . . inns, public conveyances, . . . theaters, and other places of public amusement." Penalties were likewise imposed on the denial of equal rights to serve on juries.

This law was nearly one hundred years before its time. In 1883 the Supreme Court considerably weakened the Civil Rights Act by declaring that the federal government had no power over discrimination when it was practiced by *private* persons and organizations. Private discrimination against blacks, the Court said, was legal and could not be constitutionally prevented by government action.

Nor did the Court stop there. In the landmark 1896 case of *Plessy* v. *Ferguson*, it ruled that blacks were not denied their equal rights under the Fourteenth Amendment if they were granted "separate but equal" facilities. The case had arisen in Louisiana where state law required that blacks ride in separate railroad cars from whites. If the cars for blacks were of equal quality to those enjoyed by white passengers, the Court said, then the demands of the Constitution had been satisfied and the rights of black people had not been violated.

Only one justice, John Marshall Harlan, dissented in the *Plessy* decision. The Court's action today, Harlan warned, will "stimulate aggressions, more or less brutal and irritating, upon the admitted rights of colored citizens." The "thin disguise of 'equal' accommodations," he added, "will not mislead anyone, or atone for the wrong this day done."

Harlan's dissent is worth quoting at length. "The destinies of the two races of this country," he declared, "are indissolubly linked together, and the interests of both require that the common government of all shall not permit the seeds of race hate to be planted under the sanction of law." Harlan went on to say:

What can more certainly arouse race hate, what more certainly create and perpetuate a feeling of distrust between these races, than state enactments which in fact proceed on the ground that colored citizens are so inferior and degraded that they cannot be allowed to sit in public coaches occupied by white citizens.

Harlan's dissent was prophetic. The *Plessy* decision did stimulate renewed aggressions on the rights of blacks. In 1899, three years after *Plessy*, the Supreme Court expanded the notion of "separate but equal" to include public schools. In states where black and white students were required by law to attend different schools, these laws could stand, if the schools established for the two races were equal. As A. T. Mason, a noted scholar of constitutional law, has pointed out, the Supreme Court had now "written racial segregation into the Constitution."

As a result of the "separate but equal" concept, laws requiring segregation became universal in the South and spread to other parts of the nation. The rights guaranteed by the Thirteenth, Fourteenth, and Fifteenth Amendments and the Civil Rights Act of 1876 were ignored when it came to black citizens. Blacks and whites were separated in schools, in restaurants, in rest rooms, at drinking fountains, and in every other area of society. Blacks were likewise systematically excluded from voting or holding political office.

The concept of "separate but equal" held for more than fifty years until it was knocked down by *Brown* v. *Board of Education*. On several occasions, however, the Court showed that it could defend the rights of blacks without recourse to the *Plessy* decision. In 1938 the Court ordered that a black student, Lloyd Gaines, be admitted to the all-white law school at the University of Missouri because Missouri had no law school for blacks. The state's offer to pay Gaines's fees at an out-of-state law school that accepted blacks was not sufficient, the Court said, because Gaines was a citizen of Missouri and planned to practice law there.

In 1941 and again in 1944 the Court declared that primary elections were open to the public as a whole and that blacks could not be denied the right to vote in them. And in the 1950 case of *Sweatt* v. *Painter,* it upheld a black's complaint that the Texas law school for blacks could not give him the sort of education he could receive at the white law school.

Sweatt had been denied admission to the white Texas law school solely on the basis of race. Texas officials refused him admission because educational facilities had been made available to blacks at a recently established law school in Texas. The Supreme Court, however, saw the issue differently. Writing for a unanimous Court, Chief Justice Frederick M. Vinson said that he could not find "substantial equality in the educational opportunities offered white and Negro law students by the State."

The Texas law school for whites, Vinson continued, possessed to a "far greater degree those qualities which are incapable of objective measurement but which make for greatness in a law school." These qualities were "reputation of the faculty, experience of the administration, position and influence of the alumni, standing in the community, traditions and prestige."

The Texas law school for blacks, on the other hand, had none of these qualities, and the Court ordered the white law school to admit Sweatt. The *Sweatt* decision did not overrule the "separate but equal" notion, but it challenged it. The Court recognized that the halfhearted attempts of Texas to build a black law school could not satisfy the constitutional rights of black citizens. The black school, it had declared, was obviously inferior and inadequate. From *Sweatt*, it was but one step to *Brown v. Board of Education*, which recognized the inferiority of most state attempts to give black students an education equal to that provided for whites.

The Court was not alone in the 1940s in its attempts to improve the rights of blacks. After World War II several states established committees to oversee fair and equal hiring practices by employers in their states. In 1946 President Truman established a nationwide Committee on Civil Rights, made up of leaders of both races. In 1947 the committee's report, *To Secure These Rights*, called for an end to segregation laws and the establishment of black equality.

The next year President Truman desegregated the armed forces by executive order. The tentative moves toward black equality, however, were firmly resisted by Congress. Owing to the seniority system, both the House and the Senate were dominated by southern politicians who firmly resisted any suggestions of change. As far as the southerners were concerned, segregation was the law of the land and would remain so forever.

The *Brown* Decision

The case that was to give its name to the desegregation movement came from Kansas. In 1951 Oliver Brown of Topeka sued his city's board of education on behalf of his daughter Linda. Under Kansas law, cities with more than 15,000 residents could have segregated or integrated schools. Topeka had opted for segregation.

Segregated schools meant that Linda Brown had to walk twenty blocks to the nearest all-black grade school rather than attend the all-white school in her own neighborhood. Her father believed that this was an unreasonable demand on his daughter and asked that she be admitted to the all-white neighborhood school. Several other black families of Topeka joined the case on Oliver Brown's side.

A federal district court* declared that Topeka's practice of segregation was clearly detrimental to black children. But at the same time, the district court could find no violation of the Constitution, because the black and white schools of the city were substantially equal in regard to essentials: buildings, teachers, and subjects taught. Oliver Brown, dissatisfied with the decision but heartened by the district court's statement that segregation was detrimental to blacks, decided to take his case to the Supreme Court.

When it came before the Supreme Court, *Brown* v. *Board of Education* was lumped with four other segregation cases

*There are three levels of courts in the federal judicial system. District courts are the first step, followed by circuit courts of appeal; at the third and highest level is the Supreme Court. There are about six hundred district judges, three to fourteen judges for each of the eleven appeals courts, and nine Supreme Court justices.

of a similar nature. One of these cases came from South Carolina, the others from Virginia, Delaware, and the District of Columbia. As Loren Miller, an expert on the high court's attitude towards blacks, has pointed out, "the wide geographic range" of the five cases "gave the anticipated decision a national flavor and would blunt any claim that the South was being made a whipping boy."

It is important to note, too, that in each of the five cases, the central question before the Court was the *constitutionality of segregation.* Lower federal courts had already determined that the four states in question and the District of Columbia provided equal educational facilities for blacks and whites. The issue had now become whether or not the notion of "separate but equal" satisfied the rights and needs of black Americans.

The five cases were first argued before the Court in December 1952, but six months later, in June 1953, the Court requested reargument—a sign of the importance and complexity of the issue it was deciding. Lawyers for both sides were to address themselves to three questions: Was there evidence that the Fourteenth Amendment, with its guarantees of equal rights, was intended to apply to public school segregation? Was it within the power of the Supreme Court to abolish segregation? If the Court declared segregation unconstitutional, what steps could be taken to bring it to an end?

The principal lawyer for the side challenging segregation was Thurgood Marshall. At forty-five, he was director of the NAACP Legal Defense and Educational Fund. Marshall had already argued several cases involving black rights before the Court and during his long career would argue many more for a total of thirty-two, twenty-nine of which he won. He would regard the *Brown* case, however, as his greatest triumph.

The outstanding lawyer for the other side was John W. Davis. Davis had been the Democratic candidate for President in 1924, losing to Calvin Coolidge, and had served in several high government posts. Davis was now defending the right of the states to practice segregation. Almost forty years earlier, however, in 1915, as solicitor general of the United States under Woodrow Wilson, he had convinced the Supreme Court that laws in Oklahoma that prevented blacks from voting should be declared unconstitutional. A wealthy and successful Wall Street lawyer, he had argued more cases before the Supreme Court than any other lawyer of his time.

During reargument, Davis was the first to reply to the three questions raised by the Court. His argument was strong, reflecting his experience. The Fourteenth Amendment, he claimed, had never been intended to outlaw school segregation. This was clear because several states in the North and South continued to practice segregation after the amendment was ratified. Other states had instituted segregation after ratification. Moreover, he added, several of the states practicing segregation were among those who voted for the amendment. If these states, he asked, believed that the Fourteenth Amendment required an end to segregation, would they have voted to support its ratification?

The Supreme Court, Davis said, did not have the authority to end segregation. That was the duty of the states. The "separate but equal" doctrine, he pointed out, had been upheld in case after case for more than fifty years. It had become part of the law of the land, and to overrule it now would create undue disturbance in the social fabric of the nation. Davis reminded the Court that a proper regard for *stare decisis* and tradition meant that earlier judicial decisions should not be overturned willy-nilly.

Davis likewise stated that the Supreme Court should "not sit, and cannot sit as a glorified Board of Education" for the whole United States. Lower federal courts had already concluded that in each of the five cases education offered black and white students was equivalent. If this was so, he asked, then what was the problem? All constitutional requirements had been fulfilled.

"Here is equal education," he concluded, "not promised, not prophesied, but present." Why, then, should the Supreme Court, acting like an all-powerful board of education, require the states and localities to launch an experiment in desegregation, which would, he believed, prove to be "harmful and disruptive" to all concerned?

In his reargument before the Court, Thurgood Marshall turned to a realistic assessment of American attitudes toward blacks. He likewise appealed to the principle of equality outlined in the Declaration of Independence and the Constitution. His approach contrasted vividly with the more scholarly and systematic arguments of Davis, but Marshall's statements nonetheless carried great moral weight.

In the South, Marshall said, "kids . . . play in the streets together, they play on their farms together, they go down the road together," and yet "they have to be separated in school." Why was this so? It was so, Marshall claimed, because blacks were regarded as not worthy to mix with whites in important matters, because blacks were held to be second-class citizens:

The only way that this Court can decide this case in opposition to our position, is that there must be some reason which gives the state the right to make a classification that they can make in regard to Negroes, and we submit the only way to arrive at this decision is to find that for some reason Negroes are inferior to all other human beings.

Marshall had stated the case in its starkest terms. Segregation, he believed, was practiced only to keep blacks "in their place" and somehow protect whites from "contamination." The only reason for segregation, he concluded, was to keep a people formally enslaved, or "as near that stage as possible."

Now was the time, Marshall added, for the Court to declare that segregation was "not what our Constitution stands for." It was time that the Court said for all time that the Fourteenth Amendment "was intended to deprive the states of power to enforce" segregation laws. It was time for the "separate but equal" doctrine to be struck down.

To support their case, Marshall and his assistants had assembled works by sociologists and psychiatrists that showed that segregated schools were harmful to black children. These studies—seven in number—ranged from Kenneth Clark's *Effect of Prejudice and Discrimination on Personality Development* to Swedish sociologist Gunnar Myrdal's classic work, *An American Dilemma*. The seven books argued that segregation arouses a sense of inferiority among blacks that time cannot erase.

The Court's Decision

On May 17, 1954, the nine justices appeared at the Supreme Court for the reading of the decision in *Brown* v. *Board of Education* and the related cases. One justice, Robert Jackson, left a hospital bed to be on hand for the occasion. The decision, which was read by the new chief justice, was short.

Today, Chief Justice Warren declared, the Supreme Court cannot look back to 1868, when the Fourteenth Amendment was adopted, nor can it look to 1896, when the *Plessy* decision wrote segregation into the Constitution. Rather, he said, "we must consider public education in the light of its full development and its present place in American life throughout the nation." Only in this way can we determine if public school segregation deprives blacks of "the equal protection of the laws."

"Today," he went on, "education is perhaps the most important function of state and local governments." It is the "foundation of good citizenship." It awakens the child to cultural values, prepares him or her for a profession, and helps the child "to adjust normally to his environment." So important is education, the chief justice concluded, "that it is doubtful that any child may reasonably be expected to succeed in life if he is denied the opportunity to an education."

Warren then asked the essential question: "Does segregation of children in public schools solely on the basis of race," even when all other factors might be equal, "deprive the children of the minority group of equal educational opportunities?" The Supreme Court, he said, believes that it does:

Segregation of white and colored children in public schools has a detrimental effect upon the colored children. The impact is greater when it has the sanction of law; for the policy of separating the races is usually interpreted as denoting the inferiority of the Negro group. A sense of inferiority affects the motivation of a child to learn. Segregation with the sanction of law, therefore, has a tendency to retard the educational and mental development of Negro children and to deprive them of some of the benefits they would receive in a racially integrated school system.

Then came the controversial decision. "We conclude," Warren said, "that in the field of public education the doctrine of 'separate but equal' has no place. Separate educational facilities are inherently unequal." The Court therefore held that the blacks who had brought the five cases to the Supreme Court had been "deprived of the equal protection of the laws guaranteed by the Fourteenth Amendment."

Brown II

The Court had declared segregation unconstitutional, but it postponed its decision on a remedy to segregation until the opposing sides had the opportunity to state their views. Oral arguments on remedies were heard in April 1955. Two months later, on May 31, the court announced its conclusions in what has come to be known as *Brown II*.

The chief justice first complimented three of the five litigants—Kansas, Delaware, and the District of Columbia—for having taken steps on their own to end segregation. He then pointed out that the other two states involved in the five cases—South Carolina and Virginia—were awaiting the instructions of the Court.

The Court, he declared, believes that desegregation should proceed "with all deliberate speed." The states should make "a prompt and reasonable start toward full compliance" with the original ruling in *Brown* v. *Board of Education*. "The vitality" of "the constitutional principles" involved in the case, he added, were too important to be sacrificed simply because many people disagreed with them.

The Court recognized that problems varied from state to state and that no single national plan for desegregation was practicable. It therefore returned the five cases to the lower federal courts, which had first heard them, for "judicial appraisal." Because of their closeness to local conditions, these courts could best assess the problems at hand and come up with the wisest solutions.

How were the lower federal courts to determine how much time was needed for desegregation to take place? Here the Supreme Court offered guidelines, admitting that desegregation could not take place overnight. Additional time could be granted on the basis of problems related to administration, the physical condition of the school, the school transportation system, personnel, the revision of local laws and regulations, and the revision of school districts and attendance areas "into compact units to achieve a system of admission . . . on a nonracial basis."

During the period of transition to desegregation, *Brown II* concluded, the "courts will retain jurisdiction of these cases." Any delay in the process would have to be shown to be "in the public interest" and "consistent with good faith compliance at the earliest practicable date." States and school boards, the Court implied, could not delay desegregation simply for the sake of delay.

CHAPTER THREE

The Reaction to *Brown*

Our entire way of life in this country is being revised and remolded by the nine Justices of the Supreme Court—a 1963 statement by Representative Charles H. Wilson (Democrat, California).

Response to *Brown* ran in two directions. On the one side were those who opposed the decision. They ranged from constitutional scholars who believed the Court's opinion was poorly written and reasoned—"bad law," as they called it—to out-and-out segregationists, who wanted to maintain the separation of the races.

But the response to *Brown* also had its positive side. The decision helped to stimulate and encourage the young civil rights movement. It gave hope and reassurance to blacks and other minority groups that at least one branch of government, the Supreme Court, would act to redress old grievances. Warren's activist Court had become an instrument of social change and innovation.

Brown as "Bad Law"

Many constitutional scholars and legal experts were outraged by the *Brown* decision. The decision, they argued, violated basic rules of legal tradition. Instead of coming to its conclusions on the basis of precedent and established law, the Court had largely relied on data supplied by psychologists and sociologists to buttress the conclusion that segregation was detrimental to black children.

This evidence had been carefully collected by Thurgood Marshall and his assistants, the critics pointed out, but it did not amount to *legal* evidence. Never before had the Court used this type of information to reach a major decision, and to do so now was wrong because it was too complete a break with the past. *Brown* was decided on a weak, jerry-built foundation. If the Court wanted to overturn segregation, it should have done so under clear and firm constitutional principle.

More conservative critics of *Brown* found other points to denounce. Typical of these critics was Rosalie Gordon, author of *Nine Men against America* (1958). The Court's decision, Gordon claimed, was a "totalitarian" decision that took "those last remaining bastions of a free people"—the public schools—and handed them over to the federal government. The control of schools, she maintained, was a purely local affair, not one to be decided from Washington.

What had the Supreme Court done? According to Gordon, "It did something unprecedented in our history":

It threw out the window the Constitution and all previous Court interpretations, and arrogated to itself a function reserved only for our representatives in Congress. It wrote a new law—something the Supreme Court has no right to do—and proclaimed it the law of the land by judicial fiat.

Only Congress, she pointed out, can pass laws. And it is the duty of the Court to pronounce on the constitutionality of those laws. Moreover, she claimed, if Congress *had* passed a law ending segregation, the Court would then have had to find that law unconstitutional, because Congress would have been intruding on prerogatives reserved to the states and localities.

Nor would *Brown* achieve the aims it was designed to achieve, Rosalie Gordon added. Racial issues cannot be settled by law, constitutional or otherwise. They can be settled, she concluded, only "by time and the forbearance and patience of the people involved." Had the Court left the issue alone, it would eventually have settled itself, "slowly, to be sure, in some places," but would nevertheless have come to a resolution.

Resistance to *Brown*

Rosalie Gordon spoke for those who believed the Court had violated traditions of judicial restraint and made a wrong and dangerous turn in *Brown*. Others, however, feared primarily the *social* implications of the *Brown* decision. As the historian C. Vann Woodward pointed out, "something very much like panic seized many parts of the South . . . a panic bred of insecurity and fear" as a result of the Court's order to desegregate.

Southern response took several forms. In 1955 and 1956 southern leaders began to organize a program of "massive resistance" to desegregation. Their hope was that if enough southerners ignored the Court's orders, then those orders could not be carried out. Some southern states passed laws that forbade the NAACP from operating within their borders. The legislatures of Louisiana and Mississippi ordered segregation maintained on the basis of their "police powers," which required them to promote public health and morals and protect peace and order.

Almost everywhere in the South, some means was found

to maintain segregation in public schools. Some school districts began to separate students on the basis of "scholastic ability." Others allowed students the freedom to choose which school they would attend. But whatever system was adopted, the end results were all-white schools and all-black schools.

Opposition to *Brown* was also expressed in Congress in March 1956, when 101 members of the House and Senate from southern and border states signed a "Declaration of Constitutional Principles." The declaration also came to be known as "The Southern Manifesto."

"The unwarranted decision of the Supreme Court in the public school cases," it began, "is now bearing the fruit always produced when men substituted naked power for established law. We regard the decision of the Supreme Court . . . as a clear abuse of judicial power. It climaxes a trend in the Federal Judiciary undertaking to legislate, in derogation of the authority of Congress, and to encroach upon the reserved rights of the States and the people."

The original Constitution, the declaration went on, "does not mention education. Neither does the Fourteenth Amendment nor any other Amendment." The notion of "separate but equal," upheld by the Court for more than half a century, has become "a part of the life of the people of many of the States and confirmed their habits, customs, traditions, and way of life." It is founded on "elemental humanity and common sense, for parents should not be deprived by Government of the right to direct the lives and education of their own children."

The *Brown* decision, the declaration claimed, "is creating chaos and confusion" and "has planted hatred and suspicion" between the races where there had been "friendship and understanding." In conclusion, the signers of the declaration pledged themselves "to use all lawful means to bring about a reversal of this decision which is contrary to the Constitution."

One lawful method one of the signers turned to was a constitutional amendment. Senator Herman Talmadge (Democrat, Georgia) proposed that control of the schools be turned entirely over to the local areas and that the Supreme Court be excluded by law from considering cases involving education in the public schools. Several southern leaders supported the Talmadge amendment to the Constitution, but it failed to gain substantial national support.

Little Rock

One of the most dramatic and violent reactions to *Brown* came in Little Rock, Arkansas. A few days after the *Brown* decision of 1954, the school board of Little Rock announced that it would develop a plan to desegregate the city's schools. The plan was completed a year later and called for a program of gradual desegregation that would begin in the fall of 1957 with the city's Central High School.

Before the plan could be carried out, however, the people of Arkansas, in a statewide referendum, adopted an amendment to the state constitution ordering the legislature to oppose the *Brown* decision. In response to the referendum, the legislature passed a law that allowed students in racially mixed schools in the future to ignore compulsory attendance laws.

The Little Rock school board, however, decided to continue with its desegregation plan. Nine black students were selected to enter Central High. But on September 2, 1957, the governor of Arkansas, Orval Faubus, entered the controversy by calling up the National Guard. Faubus ordered the Guard to prevent the nine black students from enrolling.

On September 4 the students attempted to enter Central High School. In spite of a federal district court order protecting their right to enroll, the students were blocked by the National Guard and by a crowd of hostile whites. For more than two weeks, Faubus continued to ignore the court order, but on September 20 he submitted and withdrew the troops.

On September 23 the nine once again tried to enroll, but had to be removed for security reasons by Little Rock police when a mob of whites became unruly and violent. Two days later the situation became so tense that President Eisenhower sent federal troops to protect the black students. The federal troops remained for more than a month, when they were replaced by federalized national guardsmen. The guard remained in Central High for the rest of the school year.

By February 1958, however, the school board had come to the conclusion that education at the high school was suffering from the continued presence of the troops and from the hostility aroused by desegregation. It asked the federal district court for permission to withdraw the blacks from school and postpone any further desegregation efforts for at least two and a half years.

The district court sympathized with the school board and granted the delay. A federal appeals court, however, reversed the district court's decision and ordered desegregation to continue without the requested postponement. The Little Rock school board then turned to the Supreme Court and renewed its request.

Believing that a decision should be handed down before the beginning of the 1958–59 school year, the Supreme

Court called a special session to hear the case, known as *Cooper v. Aaron*. Arguments for both sides were heard on September 11, and the next day the Court issued a short statement that upheld the reversal by the appeals court. This meant that desegregation in Little Rock could not be postponed.

On September 29 the Court submitted its formal decision in *Cooper v. Aaron*. The decision condemned Faubus and the Arkansas legislature for their obstructive tactics, but complimented the school board's attempts to carry out the Court's orders. The governor and the legislature, the decision pointed out, had aroused public hostility and bitterness, while the school board tried, in an orderly fashion and in "good faith" to desegregate the schools.

It should be clear to all concerned, the decision went on, that the "constitutional rights" of the black students "are not to be sacrificed or yielded to the violence and disorder which have followed upon the actions of the Governor and legislature." The Fourteenth Amendment requires that states give equal protection under law to all citizens and this, the Court implied, Arkansas has not done.

The decision then warned the opponents of desegregation that the Court would not change its mind about *Brown*. The *Brown* decision was reached unanimously "only after the case had been briefed and twice argued and the issues had been given the most serious consideration." The Court stood firmly behind *Brown* and the principles it encompassed.

Nor should the opponents of desegregation, the Court added, believe that the three new justices,* who had come

---

*The three new justices, appointed by President Eisenhower, were: *John Marshall Harlan*. Harlan was appointed to replace Justice Jackto the Court since *Brown* was handed down, suggest that there has been any weakening in the resolve of the Court. The three new justices also support *Brown* and believe that its implementation is necessary to make "our constitutional ideal of equal justice under law . . . a living truth."

In *Cooper* v. *Aaron*, the Supreme Court once again unanimously declared segregation in public schools unconstitutional. To underscore the seriousness of their commitment, all nine justices, including the three new ones, signed their names to the decision. In the face of widespread public outcry, the Court had refused to back down.

The Rights of Black Americans

The Warren Court continued to stand firm. Just as the Court's *Plessy* decision of 1896 had spawned numerous instances of legalized segregation on the basis of "separate but equal," so the *Brown* decision led to abolition of segregation in most parts of American life. The *Brown* decision had indeed started a revolution.

• *Segregation in travel and public places.* Beginning in

---

son, who had died. Harlan was the grandson of the Justice Harlan who wrote the only dissent in the case of *Plessy* v. *Ferguson.* A lifelong Republican, Harlan had served on committees investigating organized crime and the professional ethics of lawyers. He proved to be a brilliant justice and a strong advocate of judicial restraint.

William Brennan. Appointed to replace Justice Minton, who had resigned, Brennan was a Democrat from New Jersey who had served on the superior court of that state. On the Supreme Court he has been a firm supporter of liberal causes.

Charles Whittaker. Whittaker was appointed to replace Justice Reed, who had resigned. He was a Republican and a prominent lawyer from Missouri. Work on the Supreme Court, however, proved too trying, and he resigned after less than five years on the Court, complaining of exhaustion.

1954, the Court struck down the "separate but equal" doctrine when it applied to *state-imposed* segregation in public places and transportation. If segregation was unconstitutional in public schools, then it could hardly be permissible elsewhere in the public domain.

Using this argument, the Court ended discrimination in cases it considered involving public beaches, municipal golf courses, vehicles used in interstate transportation, prisons, and jails. It likewise declared unconstitutional segregation in municipal auditoriums and athletic contests, public parks, public transportation, and courtrooms.

These actions were frequently met with protest. In 1963, in the case of *Watson* v. *Memphis*, the city of Memphis asked for more time to comply with the Court's orders to desegregate its public parks and other facilities. Delay was necessary, the city argued, because rapid desegregation imposed too great a hardship on the city government and time was necessary to maintain peace and quiet during the period of transition.

The Supreme Court did not agree. The rights of all citizens to public accommodations, the Court declared, "are, like all such rights, *present* rights; they are not merely hopes to some *future* enjoyment of some formalistic constitutional promise. The basic guarantees of our Constitution are warrants for the here and now and, unless there is an overwhelmingly compelling reason, they are to be promptly fulfilled." The Court did not believe that Memphis had presented "an overwhelmingly compelling reason" for a delay in the desegregation of its parks and other facilities and denied the request for the delay.

• *The Civil Rights Act of 1964.* After the *Brown* decision of 1954, the Civil Rights Movement gained momentum. In the late 1950s and early 1960s blacks and sympathetic whites displayed their dissatisfaction with segregation through sit-ins, boycotts, marches, and demonstrations. On August 28, 1963, the movement culminated in a demonstration in Washington, D.C., by more than 200,000 people demanding equal rights for black Americans. It was the largest demonstration the capital had ever seen.

The next year Congress passed the first major and comprehensive Civil Rights Bill since 1875. The Civil Rights Bill, signed into law by President Lyndon Johnson, made a broad range of discriminatory acts unlawful. It forbade job discrimination on the basis of race, color, or national origin by employers hiring more than twenty-five employees and it gave people who believed they had been discriminated against by school boards the power to complain to the Justice Department and have their complaints investigated.

One of the more controversial aspects of the act was its prohibition of discrimination by places of business where lodgings or other public services were provided to interstate travelers. Such businesses were likewise forbidden to discriminate if a substantial proportion of the goods they sold or the entertainment they provided moved in interstate commerce.

Not long after the Civil Rights Act of 1964 was passed, the Supreme Court heard a case in which a motel owner from Atlanta, Georgia, charged that the act violated his rights as a property owner. The government, he maintained, had no right to tell him, a private citizen, how to operate his business. As a private citizen, he should have the right to choose and reject his customers without fear of government reprisal.

The case was important because it was reminiscent of an 1883 case in which the Court overturned the Civil Rights Act of 1875 because Congress, the Court claimed, had no power to interfere in acts of private discrimination. At stake now was the Civil Rights Act of 1964. Would the Court look back to the 1883 precedent and weaken the 1964 act or would it overturn the earlier precedent?

The Court upheld the 1964 act unanimously. Justice Clark wrote the decision. The Constitution, he pointed out, gave Congress the authority to regulate interstate commerce. This authority was particularly important when impediments were suffered by citizens who traveled from one state to another. In the case of blacks, he pointed out, interstate travel was particularly onerous because they did not know if they would find lodgings that would accept them. Clearly, Clark concluded, it was the duty of Congress to remove these impediments, and this is what it had attempted to do in the Civil Rights Act of 1964.

The property rights of the motel owner took second place, he implied, to the violations of "personal liberty" endured by the black travelers. He pointed out that 75 percent of the motel's clients were interstate travelers and the motel had advertised in national publications, a certain indication that it sought customers from the general public. It was precisely this type of business, Clark added, that Congress, justly and reasonably, intended to make available to all Americans, regardless of race.

• *Segregation in housing.* In a case involving discrimination in the sale of homes, the Warren Court turned back to a law passed by Congress in 1866. The case came from Missouri, where Joseph Lee Jones, solely because he was black, was denied a house he wanted to buy.

Writing the decision for a majority of seven, with two dissents, Justice Potter Stewart* argued that it was obvious

---

*Justice Stewart was Eisenhower's fifth and last appointment to the Court. He replaced Justice Burton, who resigned. A Republican and a

from the background and history of the 1866 law that it was intended to outlaw discrimination in housing when practiced privately or by the state. The law, he claimed, had been designed "to prohibit all racial discrimination, whether or not under color of the law, with respect to the rights enumerated therein—including the right to purchase or lease property."

Moreover, Stewart went on, Congress had the power to pass laws against racial discrimination, even when practiced by private individuals. This right was embodied in the Thirteenth Amendment, which had been adopted to remove "the badges of slavery" from America's blacks. One of these badges of slavery, he went on, was racial discrimination, which "herds men into ghettoes and makes their ability to buy property turn on the color of their skin." Stewart explained:

> At the very least, the freedom that Congress empowered to secure under the Thirteenth Amendment includes the freedom to buy whatever a white man can buy, the right to live wherever a white man can live. If Congress cannot say that being a free man means at least this much, then the Thirteenth Amendment made a promise the Nation cannot keep.

The Warren Court and Race Relations

The Warren Court wrote the "separate but equal" concept out of the Constitution. But more important than that, it breathed new life into the Thirteenth, Fourteenth, and

---

highly regarded lawyer, he had been a federal appeals court judge. Stewart proved to be a thoughtful justice, moderate to conservative on most issues, liberal on some.

Fifteenth Amendments, making full citizenship a possibility for millions of Americans. In its drive for equality and fairness under the law, it gave those very American ideals new meaning and weight.

During its last five years, the Warren Court considered two more significant cases involving the desegregation of public schools. The first, known as the *Griffin* case, came from Prince Edward County, Virginia. Prince Edward County had been involved in one of the five cases in the original *Brown* decision.

The county had never attempted to obey the Court's order to desegregate. Between 1955 and 1959 its schools remained segregated and were then closed. The county set up private schools for whites, supported in part by public funds. Separate private schools were offered to the county's 1,700 black students.

The black citizens, however, refused the offer of the private schools. For four years the county's "private" schools remained closed to them, and they turned to the federal judiciary for relief. In 1961 a federal court stopped the use of public funds to support the white private schools. In 1962 the same court ordered the county to reopen the public schools.

The case then went to the Supreme Court. Justice Black delivered the opinion of the Court. "There has been entirely too much deliberation," Black wrote, "and not enough speed in enforcing the constitutional rights which we held in *Brown*." These issues "imperatively call for decision now," he added and upheld the federal district court's order to reopen the schools.

The second case, known as *Green*, also came from Virginia. It involved a "freedom of choice" desegregation plan adopted by New Kent County, in which students chose the school they wanted to attend. New Kent County was not alone in this plan; other school districts had devised similar programs.

The Court unanimously rejected the freedom of choice plan. The decision was written by Justice Brennan. Brennan pointed out that it had taken New Kent County more than a decade to comply with *Brown* and that its compliance was inadequate. Under its freedom of choice plan, no white students had enrolled in all-black schools, and only 15 percent of the county's black students were attending white schools.

The plan devised by New Kent County, Brennan said, was "intolerable." It had only compounded the harm caused by segregation. The burden on the New Kent County School Board, he concluded, is to come up "with a plan that promises realistically to work, and promises realistically to work *now.*"

In both *Griffin* and *Green*, the Warren Court had characteristically stood firm on the issue of desegregation. Its firmness was a tribute to the leadership provided by the chief justice and a comment on the seriousness with which the Court as a whole regarded the *Brown* decision and its progeny. Advocates of judicial restraint deplored the activism of the Court, but others asked a question: If black Americans had waited for the normal channels of the government to work, how long would it have taken them to achieve what they achieved in a few short years after 1954?

CHAPTER FOUR

One Person, One Vote

Never in American history has a single judicial decision opened the gates for such a massive change in the nation's political structure—*Washington Post* commentator James Clayton describing the Court's 1962 decision in the case of *Baker* v. *Carr.*

Chief Justice Earl Warren did not regard *Brown* v. *Board of Education* and its offspring as the most important decisions the Supreme Court made under his leadership. More significant for him were the Court's opinions in cases involving the apportionment of state legislative and congressional districts. These decisions, he believed, corrected long-standing faults in voting practices throughout the country and ensured that every American would be equally represented in the political process.

The Problem

The 1920 census revealed that a basic change had taken place in American society. For the first time, more Americans lived in cities than in small towns or in the country. A nation that had been predominantly rural for most of its existence had now become urban. And the process of change continued. By 1960 more than 70 percent of the nation's people lived in cities, and less than 30 percent could be defined as rural.

Political institutions, however, were slow to recognize the change that had taken place. In many states, legislators and members of the House of Representatives were elected from districts that had been drawn up decades earlier, before the flight to the cities. As a result, one legislator might represent the depleted population of a rural district while another legislator represented the swollen population of an urban district, but both legislators would have the same vote in the legislature or Congress.

In 1960 studies showed that nationwide rural districts had about twice as many representatives in state legislatures as they would have had if the districts were based on population. The same studies revealed that congressional imbalance was nearly the same.

Understandably, state legislatures made no effort to clear up this disparity.* The legislatures were composed largely of legislators from rural areas who would be voting themselves out of office if an effort were made to redistrict states on the basis of new population patterns. Rural legislators feared too that if changes were made in voter representation, rural areas would soon find themselves overwhelmed and forgotten by the power of the urban vote.

Nor was help forthcoming from Congress or the Supreme Court. The Constitution gives the Congress power to override state laws regarding the election of congressmen. In 1872 Congress had used this authority to require that congressional districts throughout each state be of approximately equal size. In 1901 and 1911 it had twice again restated this requirement.

---

*As governor of California in the 1940s, Earl Warren had resisted requests for the redistricting of California based on new population patterns, even though the state's rural population was clearly overrepresented. As chief justice his views on redistricting changed enormously.

But, in a new voting law passed in 1929, Congress omitted the clause requiring equal districts, and three years later, in 1932, the Supreme Court ruled that this omission had been intentional and was to be regarded as the law of the land. The old standard of equal population no longer held. Congressional districts could be unequal.

In 1946 Kenneth Colegrove, a professor of political science at Northwestern University, decided to challenge this ruling. Colegrove's complaint was that the congressional voting districts in his home state, Illinois, were so unequal that voters in the more populous districts were denied the Fourteenth Amendment's guarantee of equal protection of the law. The difference in population between the largest district in Illinois and the smallest, Colegrove pointed out, was 800,000, a difference he found unreasonable and intolerable.

In a 4-to-3 vote, the Supreme Court rejected Colegrove's argument.* Justice Frankfurter wrote the opinion for the majority. Since Congress had omitted the requirement for equal districts from the 1929 law, he said, there were no guidelines for the Court to follow and no requirements that the states had to uphold.

But Frankfurter, the advocate of judicial restraint, found another reason for rejecting Colegrove's argument. The case, he wrote, is "of a peculiarly political nature and therefore not meet for judicial determination." The Supreme Court, he added, has "traditionally held aloof" from what he called "the political thicket." It is unwise and "hostile to a democratic system to involve the judiciary in the politics of the people."

*Justice Jackson was absent, heading the American delegation at the Nuremburg trials. Chief Justice Stone had recently died and his seat had not been filled.

Frankfurter emphasized that the authority to deal with the problem of unequal representation resided not with the Court, but "elsewhere." The Constitution gives "exclusive" power to the House of Representatives "to secure fair representation by the States . . . and left to that House determination whether States have fulfilled their responsibility." Congress, and not the Court, must deal with the problem.

Three justices—Black, Douglas, and Murphy—dissented from Frankfurter's views. The federal courts, they declared, had the power to look into cases where "federally protected rights" had been violated by state actions. Since the right to vote was clearly guaranteed by the Constitution, they concluded, the Court could have provided a "remedy to rectify the wrong done" to Colegrove.

The Court Enters the "Political Thicket"

On March 26, 1962, the Court overruled the Colegrove precedent that prevented it from considering "political" issues. The landmark case, *Baker* v. *Carr*, came from Tennessee, where voting districts had not been reorganized since 1901 even though the state's constitution required reapportionment every ten years on the basis of new population figures.

Between 1901 and 1960 Tennessee had experienced significant shifts in population from rural to urban areas, but its voting districts had remained the same. As a result, two-thirds of the members of the lower house of the legislature were elected by only 40 percent of the state's population, while two-thirds of the upper house were elected by a little more than one-third of the population.

The plaintiffs in the case argued that they and "others similarly situated" had been denied equal rights under law by the failure of the state legislature to redistrict. The plaintiffs, who were residents of urban areas, also contended that the value of their votes had been debased, because they were underrepresented in state government, while rural residents were overrepresented.

The question before the Court was whether voters whose right to vote had been diluted by unfair or unequal apportionment could seek relief in the federal courts. A majority of six justices answered with a resounding yes. Distinguishing between "political rights" and "political questions," Justice Brennan argued that the Court had the authority to consider violations of the former without getting involved in the latter. Political questions, he implied, are rightly left to other branches of government. A case concerning a transgression against political rights guaranteed in the Constitution, however, is clearly in the jurisdiction of the Court.

Justice Clark, who wrote a concurring opinion, agreed. The Court, he believed, had a judicial duty to consider the question of valid apportionment. "I would not consider intervention by this Court," he wrote, "into so delicate a field if there were any other relief available to the people of Tennessee. But the majority of the people of Tennessee have no practical opportunities for exerting their political weight at the polls."

It was all well and good for the Court to practice judicial restraint, Clark added, and look to the popularly elected legislatures to remedy injustice. But the Supreme Court, he went on, has never relied on judicial restraint "where the national rights of so many have been so clearly infringed for so long a time." Clark believed that it was up to the Court to remedy the apportionment problem in Tennessee, because the legislature had shown time and time again that it would not.

Equality in Voting Power

In the *Baker* case the Court asserted the authority to consider apportionment problems. In 1963, the year following *Baker*, the Court adopted the phrase "one person, one vote" to describe the ideal it strove for in voting districts. The case of *Gray* v. *Sanders* came from Georgia, where a "county-unit" primary system was used in the election of state officials. The system was heavily weighted in favor of rural counties and gave them a distinct electoral advantage over Georgia's urban population.

The Supreme Court declared, 8 to 1, that the county-unit system was unconstitutional. Justice Douglas wrote the opinion for the majority. "How then," asked Douglas, "can one person be given twice or ten times the voting power of another person in a statewide election merely because he lives in a rural area or because he lives in the smallest rural county?"

The phrase "We the people," which opens the Preamble to the Constitution, he went on, "visualized no preferred class of voters but equality among those who meet the basic qualification. The idea that every voter is equal to every other voter in his state . . . underlies" many decisions the Court has handed down. Indeed, he concluded, it underlies the whole of American history: "The conception of political equality from the Declaration of Independence to Lincoln's Gettysburg Address, to the Fifteenth, Seventeenth, and Nineteenth Amendments can mean only one thing—one person, one vote."*

*The Fifteenth Amendment gave male citizens the right to vote, regardless of "race, color, or previous condition of servitude." The Sev-

In 1964, in two separate cases, the Court applied the idea of one person, one vote first to congressional districts and then to districts electing delegates to both houses of state legislatures. The congressional district case, *Wesberry v. Sanders*, came from Georgia. The case involving state legislative districts, *Reynolds* v. *Sims*, came from Alabama.

The question behind *Wesberry* was a complaint from voters in Georgia's fifth congressional district. The fifth district, they pointed out, held more than twice as many people as it should, if the state's average of 394,312 persons per congressional district was taken into consideration. The enormous size of the district, they added, meant that its voters lacked adequate representation in the House of Representatives.

In a 6-to-3 decision, the Supreme Court decided in favor of the voters of the fifth district. Justice Black wrote the majority decision, which offered guidelines for lower federal courts to follow in other congressional reapportionment cases. In its "historical context," wrote Black, the command in the Constitution that representatives be elected "by the people of the several States" means that "as nearly as is practicable, one man's vote in a congressional election is to be worth as much as another's."

Black acknowledged that it might not be possible to draw congressional districts with "mathematical precision." But he stressed that the inability to attain precision was "no excuse for ignoring our Constitution's plain objective of making equal representation for equal numbers the fundamental goal of the House of Representatives."

enteenth established the direct election of senators by the people rather than by state legislatures. The Nineteenth gave women the right to vote.

In *Reynolds* v. *Sims*, the Court applied the principle of one person, one vote to state legislatures. It was this case that Chief Justice Warren regarded as the most important of his career, and it was Warren who wrote the decision for the Court's 8-to-1 majority.

"The right to vote freely for the candidate of one's choice," the chief justice wrote, "is of the essence of a democratic society, and any restrictions on that right strike at the heart of representative government." When a citizen's vote is thinned down by unequal voting districts, Warren maintained, his right to vote has been denied as effectively as if he had been denied the right to vote altogether:

> Legislators represent people, not trees or acres. Legislators are elected by voters, not farms or cities or economic interests. As long as ours is a representative form of government, and our legislatures are those instruments of government elected directly by and directly representative of the people, the right to elect legislators in a free and unimpaired fashion is a bedrock of our political system.

"The weight of a citizen's vote," Warren concluded, "cannot be made to depend on where he lives."

Warren pointed out that the state of Alabama, where the case under question had arisen, argued that it had the right to constitute its legislature as the federal government did, with one house based on population, like the House of Representatives, and one on area, like the Senate. But the chief justice rejected this argument. The analogy between state and federal governments, he said, did not hold up.

When the Constitution established Congress, he maintained, the states were independent, sovereign units entitled to the two types of representation granted the House and Senate. But counties and divisions of states had never known this degree of independence and sovereignty and were mere units of political and administrative convenience. Counties, he concluded, could not be regarded in the same league as the states.

After rejecting the federal analogy, Warren declared that "both houses of a state legislature must be apportioned on a population basis." Establishing apportionment on any other basis impairs an individual's right to suffrage. The constitutional promise of equal protection under law, he added, "requires that a State make an honest and good faith effort to construct districts, in both houses of its legislature, as nearly equal in population as is practicable."

For the present, Warren deemed it "expedient" for the Court not to spell out precise requirements for reapportionment. What might work in one state would not work in another. The federal courts would therefore approach state legislative reapportionment on a case-by-case basis.

Warren did, however, believe that more flexibility would be granted the states in the reapportionment of legislative districts than in the reapportionment of congressional districts. "We realize that it is a practical impossibility," he concluded, "to arrange legislative districts so that each one has an identical number of residents, or citizens, or voters." In the case of congressional districts, however, he believed that the constitutional mandate for equality was more severe and that therefore the standards established by the Court had likewise to be more severe.

Dissent

The Warren Court's reapportionment decisions were not unanimously approved by the Court. Justice Frankfurter and Justice Harlan issued strong dissents in the *Baker* case, in which the Court declared the question of reapportionment within its jurisdiction, and Justice Harlan issued equally vigorous dissents in the cases establishing the doctrine of one person, one vote.*

Frankfurter thought it was obvious that the Court, in at least a dozen cases, had rejected the right to consider political questions like reapportionment. He reminded the justices of his majority opinion in the 1946 Colegrove case in which he had warned about entering the "political thicket." That warning, he said, was as meaningful now as it was when it was written.

The *Baker* case, he concluded, was a "massive repudiation of the experience of our whole past" and amounted to an assertion of a new destructive power on the part of the Court. Judges are not "omnicompetent," he went on, and should not be given power that rightly belongs to the legislatures of the fifty states or to Congress.

There is no doubt that the state legislatures have failed to carry out responsibilities assigned to them, he implied. But the Court is wrong in believing that there is "under our Constitution a judicial remedy for every political mischief, for every undesirable exercise of legislative power."

Justice Harlan agreed. "What the Court is doing" in accepting jurisdiction in a reapportionment case, he said, "reflects more an adventure in judicial experimentation than

*In 1962, after the *Baker* case was handed down, Justice Frankfurter retired. President John Kennedy appointed Arthur Goldberg to replace him. Justice Goldberg was a Democrat with an impressive background in labor law. On the Court, he proved to be a liberal and activist justice. Also in 1962 Justice Whittaker retired, and President Kennedy appointed his friend, Byron White, to the Court. White was a highly regarded Colorado lawyer, who had been a professional football player for one year with the Pittsburgh Steelers. On the Court, he proved to be a moderate.

a solid piece of constitutional adjudication." Nothing in the Constitution, Harlan concluded, gave the Court the permission to do what it had done.

In his dissents in the cases involving the notion of one person, one vote Harlan continued in this vein. The Court's claims for a constitutional right to equal representation, he wrote, have been "manufactured out of whole cloth" and have no basis in tradition. Moreover, he added, the Court's pronouncements on reapportionment were "profoundly ill-advised"—the product of "a current mistaken view of the Constitution and the constitutional function of this Court."

What was this mistaken view Harlan believed the Warren Court held?

This view, in a nutshell, is that every major social ill in this country can find its cure in some constitutional "principle," and that this Court should "take the lead" in promoting reform when other branches of government fail to act. The Constitution is not a panacea for every blot upon the public welfare, nor should this Court, ordained as a judicial body, be thought of as a haven for reform movements.

Why did Harlan believe reapportionment to be ill-advised? Because, he wrote, the Court's participation in reapportionment cuts "deeply into the fabric of our federalism." However desirable it might be to require the states to establish more equitable districts, the cost is too high because it involves "a radical alteration in the relationship between the States and the Federal Government, more particularly the Federal Judiciary."

Harlan's views were a reiteration of Jefferson's attacks on Chief Justice Marshall more than one hundred fifty years earlier. Both Harlan and Jefferson deplored what they saw as the Court's attack on states' rights and federalism, and both men feared the tendency of an activist Court to assume more and more power.

Reaction

The Supreme Court's reapportionment decisions aroused widespread controversy. One group that voiced concern was the Council of State Governments, an organization dedicated to the preservation of states' rights. In February 1973, a year after the *Baker* decision, the council proposed a constitutional amendment that would take reapportionment out of the hands of the Supreme Court and return it to the states.

The amendment likewise proposed that a Court of the Nation, composed of the chief justices of the fifty states, be established to consider and review the decisions of the U. S. Supreme Court. Nothing came of the council's proposals, but the drastic nature of the solution its amendment offered reveals the degree of dissatisfaction aroused by the Court's entry into the "political thicket" of reapportionment.

More significant was the constitutional amendment proposed by Senator Everett Dirksen (Republican, Illinois). The Dirksen amendment took reapportionment away from the courts and returned it to the states, allowing the states to establish legislatures on the basis of the federal analogy: a lower house based on population, an upper house based on "population, geography, and political subdivisions in order to insure effective representation in the state's legislature of the various groups and interests making up the electorate."

In spite of Dirksen's enormous prestige, the amendment failed to pass the Senate when it was offered in 1965. By

1969, however, he had succeeded in getting the approval of all but one of the state legislatures needed to call a constitutional convention to consider the amendment. The momentum for change, however, by that time had died out.

Unlike the *Brown* decision, whose effect was primarily on the South and the border states where segregation was practiced by law, the Court's reapportionment decisions affected every part of the nation. In May 1966 the Council of State Governments reported that thirty-seven states, under federal court orders, had reapportioned one or more houses of their legislatures. Urban districts, long underrepresented, found their needs and concerns heard for the first time.

When new plans for reapportionment came up for consideration, the Court required very strict adherence to equality of representation in the case of congressional districts—at one time turning down a Missouri plan whose largest variation between districts was 3.1 percent—but was less strict in adherence to the equality standard in cases involving legislative districts. In 1972, in the first congressional election following reapportionment on the basis of the 1970 census, 385 of the 435 members of the House of Representatives were elected from districts that varied in population less than *1 percent* from the population of other congressional districts in their state.

CHAPTER FIVE

The Warren Court and the Rights of the Accused

It is a shame to think there should be one law for the poor and one for the rich—Chief Justice Earl Warren.

Another problem taken up by the Warren Court was criminal justice. Here too the Court intruded into areas of law traditionally regarded as belonging to the states. Before Warren, federal courts had one system of criminal procedure, while the states had others, which varied from state to state. Federal courts were required to adhere to criminal rights found in the Bill of Rights, which state courts were free to ignore.

During the 1960s, in case after case, the Warren Court overturned this double system of justice and extended to state courts the same requirements already placed on federal courts. The change was made in the name of fairness and equality and in order to establish a consistent, unified criminal procedure for the entire nation. Critics, however, believed that the Court's decisions were ill-advised because they tended to hamper the work of police and "pamper criminals" at a time when the country's crime rate was on the rise.

• • •

The Warren Court and Fourth Amendment Rights

The Fourth Amendment guarantees that "The right of the people to be secure in their persons, houses, papers, and effects, against unreasonable searches and seizures, shall not be violated." To help protect this right against "unreasonable searches and seizures," the amendment stipulates that no warrants shall be issued, except "upon probable cause, supported by oath or affirmation, and particularly describing the place to be searched, and the persons or things to be seized."

In 1914, on the basis of this Amendment, the Supreme Court declared that evidence taken as a result of "unreasonable searches and seizures" had to be excluded from federal court trials. Such evidence, the Court said, involved "a denial of the constitutional rights of the accused" and to admit it as proof of guilt in a criminal trial would be a violation of the "fundamental law of the land." From that time on, federal law officials were required to adhere strictly to the Fourth Amendment's command against unreasonable searches.

The command against unreasonable search and seizure, however, did not pertain to state or local law officials. State courts continued to accept evidence that had been taken in violation of the Fourth Amendment and to regard it as acceptable proof of guilt in criminal trials, where state law permitted. The Fourth Amendment was regarded as federal law, not applicable to the states.

On June 19, 1961, the Supreme Court, in the case of *Mapp* v. *Ohio*, handed down a decision that directly challenged this practice. Dollree Mapp, the plaintiff, had been convicted of possession of obscene literature. The evidence against her had been taken by police who had forced their way into her home, without a warrant.

The police were acting on a tip that a person they wanted for questioning was hiding in Dollree Mapp's home and that illegal gambling equipment was hidden there. The obscene material that resulted in her conviction was found as a result of a complete search of her home.

Dollree Mapp complained that her rights as a citizen of the United States had been violated. The question before the Court was clear: Did the Fourth Amendment's prohibition of unreasonable searches apply to this case and should the evidence obtained in the search of Dollree Mapp's home be excluded from a state court trial because it had been illegally obtained?

In a 6-to-3 decision the Supreme Court declared that the evidence should be excluded. Justice Clark wrote the opinion for the majority. The "right to privacy" guaranteed by the Fourth Amendment, Clark maintained, is extended to the states by the Fourteenth Amendment, which says that no state shall "deprive any person of life, liberty, or property, without due process of law." The evidence against Mapp, he added, had been "secured by official lawlessness in flagrant abuse" of basic rights. Clearly, she had been denied "due process of law."

The states must be required to exclude illegally obtained evidence from state trials, Clark went on, because to do otherwise would tend "to destroy the entire system of constitutional restraints on which the liberties of the people rest." Police officers must no longer be permitted to conduct unreasonable searches and seizures on whim. The same strictures placed on federal law officers must likewise be placed on state law officials.

The Warren Court and Sixth Amendment Rights

The Sixth Amendment states that "In all criminal prosecutions, the accused shall enjoy the right . . . to have the assistance of counsel for his defense." A literal reading of the amendment would seem to indicate that all defendants in criminal cases are required to be represented by an attorney, even if they are too poor to pay for one.

In most of American history, however, this has not been true. Only in 1938 did the Supreme Court require that all federal defendants be provided an attorney. State defendants, meanwhile, were required to have attorneys only in cases punishable by death or when "special circumstances"—such as illiteracy or mental illness—necessitated the aid of counsel.

In 1963 the Warren Court expanded the right to counsel in its decision in the case of *Gideon* v. *Wainwright*. Clarence Earl Gideon had been arrested for a felony—breaking and entering a poolroom—by Florida police. An indigent, he could not afford a lawyer and asked the court to appoint a counsel to act in his defense.

The judge denied Gideon's request in these words: "Mr. Gideon, I am sorry, but I cannot appoint Counsel to represent you in this case. Under the laws of the state of Florida, the only time the Court can appoint Counsel . . . is when that person is charged with a capital offense." The defendant attempted to conduct his own defense, but was convicted and sentenced to five years in prison. While in prison, Gideon studiously prepared his own petitions, asking higher courts to declare his conviction invalid because he had been refused his constitutional right to counsel. He exhausted the Florida appeals procedures and turned to the federal courts.

When his case reached the Supreme Court, the Court appointed the successful and well-known Washington attorney, Abe Fortas, to act in Gideon's behalf. By that time, 1962, Gideon's case had become famous. Twenty-two states filed "friends of the court" briefs with the high court urging that the "right to counsel" be made a constitutional requirement for the states. The American Civil Liberties Union likewise filed a brief on Gideon's behalf.

Justice Hugo Black wrote the decision for a unanimous Court in the case of *Gideon* v. *Wainwright*. It was clear, Black declared, that Gideon had been denied his constitutional rights. The right-to-counsel provision of the Sixth Amendment, he said, was "fundamental and essential to a fair trial." Without a lawyer, a poor defendant could not be guaranteed equal treatment under the law.

The "right of one charged with crime to counsel may not be deemed fundamental and essential to a fair trial in some countries," Black went on, "but it is in ours. . . . From the very beginning, our state and national constitutions and laws have laid great emphasis on procedural and substantive safeguards designed to assure fair trials before impartial tribunals in which every defendant stands equal before the law."

"This noble ideal," he concluded, "cannot be realized if the poor man charged with crime has to face his accusers without a lawyer to assist him." The right to counsel is a necessity, not a luxury.

The Warren Court and the Right to Remain Silent

Among other things, the Fifth Amendment stipulates that "No person . . . shall be compelled in any criminal case to be a witness against himself." This privilege is often referred to as the "right to remain silent." In the case of *Escobedo* v. *Illinois* (1964), the Warren Court turned to a defendant's right to remain silent and linked this right to the right to counsel, already established in the *Gideon* decision of the year before.

Danny Escobedo, the plaintiff, had been arrested for murder. During his police interrogation, he repeatedly asked for the aid of his lawyer, but was denied this aid. During his trial, statements he had made during the interrogation were used against him and he was found guilty. Escobedo challenged the conviction, arguing that because his right to counsel had been violated, his trial had not been fair and impartial.

A Court divided 5 to 4 decided in favor of Escobedo. Justice Arthur Goldberg wrote the decision for the majority: What bothered the Court, Goldberg explained, were the details of the police interrogation. At the time of the arrest and during the period of questioning, the police had told Escobedo that they had "convincing evidence" that he had committed the crime and urged him to make a statement.

But at no time, Goldberg continued, did the police inform the defendant that he had the "absolute right" to remain silent. Ignorant of his basic rights, Escobedo had been led to make statements that were later used against him. Clearly, Goldberg maintained, the "guiding hand of counsel" had been needed to provide Escobedo with advice on his rights "in this delicate situation."

The period of interrogation, Goldberg went on, was the "stage when legal aid advice" was most critical for the defendant, because what had happened during the interrogation affected his whole trial. The *Gideon* decision, he pointed out, had guaranteed the right to counsel in serious crimes. But this right would be hollow and insignificant if a confession of guilt had already been taken from the accused.

The Court believes, Goldberg concluded, that when the process of criminal investigation shifts from the investigatory stage to the accusatory—"when its focus is on the accused and its purpose is to elicit a confession"—then the defendant must be informed both of his right to remain silent and of his right to counsel. These rights, he added, were operative not only in federal courts but also in state criminal law because of the Fourteenth Amendment's command that no state could deprive a citizen of due process of law.

The Court also holds, Goldberg said, that if the defendant is not informed of his rights, then any information taken from him during the police interrogation cannot be used against him. "No system worth preserving," he explained, "should have to *fear* that if an accused is permitted to consult with a lawyer, he will become aware of, and exercise," his right to remain silent or his right to counsel. "If the exercise of constitutional rights will thwart the effectiveness of a system of law enforcement, then there is something very wrong with that system."

Miranda v. Arizona

The most controversial criminal-procedure decision handed down by the Warren Court was *Miranda* v. *Arizona* (1966). In *Miranda* the Court established "concrete constitutional guidelines" for police to follow in the interrogation of the accused. The decision aroused the bitter resentment of critics who believed that it intruded unreasonably into the work of police and prevented them from carrying out that work effectively.

Ernesto Miranda was tried for kidnapping and rape in Arizona. Statements he made after his arrest and during police interrogation were used against him, and he was convicted and imprisoned. Before they interrogated him, however, the police had failed to advise him of his right to remain silent and his right to counsel. From prison, Miranda challenged his conviction, saying that the evidence used against him had been illegally obtained because his constitutional rights had been violated.

The Supreme Court split 5 to 4 in favor of Miranda. Chief Justice Warren wrote the opinion for the majority. The *Miranda* case, the chief justice claimed, raises "questions which go to the root of American criminal jurisprudence." What were these questions? They involved, he continued, "the constraints society must observe consistent with the federal Constitution in prosecuting individuals for crime."

Above all, Warren argued, criminal interrogations and prosecutions should be handled in a way that allows the accused to maintain his human dignity. The problem arose because of the way in which police conducted their interrogations. Questioning was carried on in privacy. The suspect was alone with the police, who employed "patience and persistence" and "at times, relentless questioning." As a result, the defendant's "will to resist is undermined and he is deprived of outside support."

Moreover, Warren argued, when "normal procedures" fail to get results, the police interrogators may turn to other methods. They may offer false legal advice that misleads the accused. "The police then persuade, trick, or conjole him" out of exercising his constitutional rights or use some other means "to keep the subject off balance" and trade on his "insecurity about himself and his surroundings."

"This atmosphere," the chief justice declared, "carries its own badge of intimidation. To be sure, this is not physical intimidation, but it is equally destructive of human dignity":

> The current practice of incommunicado interrogation is at odds with one of our Nation's most cherished principles—that the individual may not be compelled to incriminate himself. Unless adequate protective devices are employed to dispel the compulsion inherent in custodial surroundings, no statement obtained from the defendant can truly be said to be the product of his free choice.

What were the "protective devices" that the police could employ to assure the defendant of his constitutional rights and freedom of choice? Warren listed two. First, "at the outset, if a person in custody is to be subjected to interrogation, he must first be informed in clear and unequivocal terms that he has the right to remain silent." Second, "the warning of the right to remain silent must be accompanied by the explanation that anything said can and will be used against the individual in court."

This warning, the chief justice explained, is needed in order to make the suspect aware of his privileges and the consequences of turning those privileges down. Once he has been warned, then he must be told that he has the right to the presence of an attorney and "that if he cannot afford an attorney one will be appointed for him prior to any questioning if he so desires." Only when he "knowingly and intelligently" rejects the warning and the offer of counsel does the defendant lose these rights.

If "at any stage" of the interrogation process, Warren added, the defendant indicates "in any manner" that he wishes to consult with a lawyer, there can be no further questioning. "The mere fact that he may have answered some questions," the chief justice concluded, ". . . does not deprive him of the right to refrain from answering any further inquiries until he has consulted with an attorney and thereafter consents to be questioned."

Dissent

The *Gideon* decision, extending the right of counsel, had been unanimous. In the other criminal cases, however, the Court was severely divided. In *Mapp* the Court voted 6 to 3; in *Escobedo* and *Miranda* it split 5 to 4. The Warren Court was unable to maintain the unanimity it had displayed in cases involving race relations or the near-unanimity it showed in the early reapportionment cases.

Justice Harlan's dissent in *Mapp* revealed his basic distrust of the venture the Court was making into the problem of criminal procedure. For the Supreme Court, he argued, to declare that state courts had to abide by the same rules as federal courts and exclude illegally obtained evidence from trials was a violation of American judicial tradition. It showed that the Court had "forgotten the sense of judicial restraint" and no longer possessed a "due regard for *stare decisis.*"

But Harlan's dissent in *Mapp* was mild in comparison with the dissents he and the other three dissenting justices registered in *Escobedo* and *Miranda*. According to Justice White, the *Escobedo* opinion was a perversion and distortion of the constitutional rights it sought to guarantee. Moreover, it had the added effect of frustrating "the legitimate and proper function of honest and purposeful police investigation."

To require that a defendant be granted his right to counsel as soon as he began to be regarded as a suspect in a criminal case, White pointed out, was to require a "rule wholly unworkable and impossible to administer unless police cars are equipped with public defenders and undercover agents and police informants have defense counsel at their side."

The new rule, he continued, "is perhaps thought to be a necessary safeguard against the possibility of extorted confessions." But this reveals, he maintained, that the Court has a "deep-seated distrust of law enforcement officers everywhere." This distrust is not supported by "relevant data or current material based upon our own experience."

Obviously, he acknowledged, law officers "can make mistakes and exceed their authority, but I have somewhat more faith than the Court evidently has in the ability and desire of prosecutors and the power of the appellate courts to discern and correct such violations of the law."

The *Escobedo* decision, White concluded, was "nebulous" and stood "as an impenetrable barrier to any interrogation once the accused has become a suspect." How then could meaningful police work take place? "For unsound, unstated reasons, which can find no home in any of the provisions of the Constitution," *Escobedo* has rendered criminal justice more difficult to obtain.

Justice Harlan took a similar position in his dissent in the *Miranda* decision. Now the prime advocate of judicial restraint on the Court, Harlan wrote that he believed that "the decision of the Court represents poor constitutional law and entails harmful consequences for the country at large." To incorporate the new decision into the Constitution, he claimed, "requires a strained reading of history and precedent and a disregard of the very pragmatic concerns that alone may on occasion justify such strains."

Why did he believe that the decision entailed "harmful consequences" for the nation? Harlan pointed out that the *Miranda* rules written by Chief Justice Warren were not designed to guard against police brutality or "other unmistakably banned forms of coercion." Any police official who employed brutal methods of interrogation would be equally able to lie about his behavior, so any rule or constitutional ban would be unable to reach him.

Rather, Harlan went on, the effect of the *Miranda* rules "is to negate all pressures, to reinforce the nervous or ignorant suspect, and ultimately to discourage any confession at all." The Court, he concluded, "is taking a real risk with society's welfare in imposing its new" rules for criminal procedure on the nation. "The social costs of crime are too great to call the new rules anything but a hazardous experimentation."

Positive and Negative Response

Response to the Court's *Gideon* decision, which established the right to counsel in all serious crimes, was generally positive. Most Americans believed that it was important to ensure that all defendants be given the opportunity to have a fair trial. President John Kennedy recommended that Congress pass a Criminal Justice Act to provide counsel for the poor and indigent in federal courts. In 1964, the year after Kennedy's assassination, the act passed Congress and was signed into law by President Johnson.

The response to the Court's other criminal-justice decisions and especially to *Escobedo* and *Miranda*, however, was widespread and bitter. Representatives of police organizations and other law enforcement groups complained that the actions of the Court had considerably hampered police activities and made it difficult to deal with the country's growing crime rate.

In 1968 the Omnibus Crime Control and Safe Streets Act came up for consideration in Congress. Included in the Act was a provision specifically designed to moderate the effect of the *Miranda* rules. By allowing federal court judges to permit the use of voluntary confessions as evidence in criminal trials, Congress hoped to overrule the more severe procedural guidelines outlined in *Miranda.*

The debate over the bill in the Senate revealed the depth of the controversy aroused by the Court's decision. Speaking in support of the bill, Senator John McClellan (Democrat, Arkansas) declared, "The true issue, and there is no escaping it, is the spiraling rate of crime and the erroneous decisions of the Supreme Court versus the safety of our people and the security of our country." America cannot have at the same time, he implied, both the Warren Court and social stability and well-being. The five members of the Court who formed the majority in *Escobedo* and *Miranda,* he concluded, simply had no respect for the Constitution.

McClellan then linked the Court's decisions to the crime rate. If the congressional bill limiting the court's rulings was not passed, he warned, then organized crime and "every murderer, rapist, robber, burglar, arsonist, thief, and con man will have cause to rejoice and celebrate." But "every innocent, law-abiding, and God-fearing citizen in this land will have cause to weep and despair."

Speaking against the crime bill, Senator Joseph Tydings (Democrat, Maryland) took issue with McClellan. The *Miranda* decision, he pointed out, did not benefit organized crime; organized crime already had enough money to pay for the best lawyers available. *Miranda* and the other criminal-procedure decisions, Tydings maintained, were simply an effort on the part of the Court to ensure that everyone, including the poor and ignorant, shared the same constitutional rights.

McClellan's side won. The Omnibus Crime Control and Safe Streets Act passed the Congress and was signed into law by the President. Title II of the act gave federal court judges the power to determine the admissibility of confessions taken during police interrogations. Title II affected only trials in federal courts, while the *Miranda* procedures still held for state courts.

The controversy raised by the *Escobedo* and *Miranda* decisions entered the presidential campaign of 1968. Richard Nixon, running for the presidency on the Republican ticket, strongly attacked the Warren Court for what he regarded as its liberal interpretation of the Constitution and its pampering of criminals.

He promised the nation that if he was elected President he would appoint justices who respected "law and order" and shared his belief in a "strict interpretation of the Constitution." Nixon made good his promise. With the retirement of Chief Justice Earl Warren in 1969, the new President had his first opportunity to alter the direction of the Court. For chief justice, Nixon turned to Warren E. Burger, a man who had come to his notice as a staunch critic of the Warren Court's criminal-procedure decisions.

CHAPTER SIX

The Warren Court and Religion

> Can it be that we, too, are ready to embrace the foul concept of atheism? . . . Is this not in fact the first step on the road to prompt atheistic and agnostic beliefs? . . . Somebody is tampering with America's soul. I leave to you who that somebody is—Senator Robert Byrd (Democrat, West Virginia) in response to the Supreme Court's banning of prayer and Bible reading in public schools.

> Under the present Chief Justice, the Court has undoubtedly done more to strengthen the rights of the individual than it ever did in all the years up to his appointment—Editorial in the *San Francisco Chronicle*, 1966.

In 1963 and 1964 the Warren Court declared prayer and Bible reading in public schools unconstitutional. The controversy set off by the two decisions still rages today. The Court believed it had based its decisions on a fair reading of the Constitution and a due regard for individual rights. Critics, however, charged that the Court had become an enemy of traditional religion and was trying to impose its own secularist beliefs on the American people.

The Problem

The first right mentioned in the Bill of Rights is freedom of religion. "Congress shall make no law respecting an establishment of religion," the First Amendment states, "or prohibiting the free exercise thereof." The amendment ensures the separation of church and state. No one religion can be designated as the national religion of the United States, nor can the government interfere in the practice of religious faith.

The American attitude toward religion, however, is double-edged. On the one side, the United States prides itself on the separation of church and state and regards this separation as essential to American democracy. America, this argument runs, is a land where any number of religions can flourish and develop.

On the other hand, Americans have always regarded themselves as a religious people and have believed that American history was closely linked with religious faith. American currency carries the inscription "In God We Trust" and the Pledge of Allegiance contains the phrase "one nation, under God." In addition, both Congress and the Supreme Court have traditionally been opened by prayer or other religious observances.

The problem, then, has been to reconcile the separation of church and state with the firm religious convictions of most Americans without doing damage to either tradition. This was the dilemma faced by the high court in its two controversial decisions on school prayer and Bible reading. How could the notion that religion and the state should not be mixed be balanced with the belief that religion should nevertheless play an important part in national life?

The School Prayer Decision

The school prayer case, known as *Engel* v. *Vitale*, came from the state of New York. The New York Board of Regents, an agency that ran the state's public schools, composed a nondenominational prayer. The board recommended that the state's school districts adopt the prayer, which could be recited voluntarily at the beginning of each school day. Students who did not wish to recite the prayer were not to be required to do so.

The prayer was short and concise: "Almighty God, we acknowledge our dependence upon Thee, and we beg Thy blessings upon us, our parents, our teachers, and our country." Some of the state's school districts chose to reject the prayer. New York City, for example, replaced it with a verse from the patriotic song, "America," which asks for God's blessings and protection on the nation. Many New York school districts, however, found the prayer acceptable and began to put it into daily use.

The first challenge to the prayer came from the city of New Hyde Park, a Long Island suburb of New York City. The parents of ten pupils brought suit in a state court, claiming that the use of the prayer was "contrary to the beliefs, religions, or religious practices of both themselves and their children." The suit was supported by the New York Civil Liberties Union.

The parents charged that "the prayer was composed by governmental officials as a part of a governmental program to further religious beliefs" and therefore a violation of the First Amendment injunction against the establishment of religion. It was unconstitutional, they argued, for a state to authorize a prayer for use in public schools and for school boards to order recitation of the prayer, even on a voluntary basis.

The New York courts rejected the claims of the parents and upheld the use of the prayer, as long as no student was compelled to recite it who had asked not to. But the U. S.

Supreme court overturned the state court decision and declared use of the prayer unconstitutional by a vote of 6 to 1. Justice Hugo Black, an ardent defender of First Amendment rights, wrote the decision for the majority.

"There can be no doubt," Black wrote, "that New York's state prayer program officially establishes the religious beliefs embodied in the Regents' prayer." The prayer in question, he added, is clearly a "religious activity." It is also "a solemn avowal of divine faith and supplication for the blessings of the Almighty."

Black rejected the argument that since the prayer was "nondenominational" it should be acceptable to all. He likewise rejected the notion that since it was voluntary, the prayer did not violate the religious beliefs of minorities. When the "power" and "prestige" of the government of New York were put behind the prayer, he pointed out, then the prayer became something more than "neutral." It became an official pronouncement of the state.

The Supreme Court, Black continued, holds that the prayer is unconstitutional and must not be used in public schools. It is unconstitutional, he explained, because "the constitutional prohibition against laws respecting establishment of religion must at least mean that in this country it is no part of the business of government to compose official prayers for any group of the American people to recite as a part of a religious program carried on by government."

Black went on to point out the reason behind the First Amendment's guarantee of religious freedom and its prohibition of established religion. The "first and most immediate purpose" of the amendment, he said, "rested on the belief that a union of government and religion tends to destroy government and to degrade religion." The amendment "stands as an expression of principle on the part of the Founders of our Constitution that religion is too personal, too sacred, too holy, to permit its 'unhallowed perversion' by a civil magistrate."

Black then added that America was in part settled by colonists who were fleeing the established religion of England to practice their own faiths in the New World. They were escaping, he claimed, a society where "governmentally composed prayers" were part of a national religion and where religious freedom was impossible. For the Supreme Court now to accept a state-composed prayer, he implied, would be a rejection of some of the most valuable traditions that had formed American life.

Justice Black stressed that the Court's decision did not reflect a "hostility" toward religion. "Nothing," he wrote, "could be more wrong." Religion had always played an important part in the history of humanity and would continue to do so. But "it is neither sacriligious nor antireligious," Black concluded, to say that government in America "should stay out of the business of writing or sanctioning official prayers." That business should be left "to the people themselves and to those the people choose to look to for religious guidance."

As for those who believed that the New York prayer was so "brief and general" that it offered no challenge to religious freedom, Black asked them to turn to the words of James Madison,* the Founding Father who was the "author of the First Amendment." "It is proper," Madison once

*In his book, *The American Constitution*, C. Hermann Pritchett points out that Madison's attitude toward the prohibition of established religion was absolute. Both Madison and Jefferson, for instance, believed that it would be improper for the President to issue a proclamation on Thanksgiving Day because the proclamation would constitute state involvement in a religious exercise.

wrote, "to take alarm at the first experiment on our liberties":

Who does not see that the same authority which can establish Christianity, in exclusion of all other Religions, may establish with the same ease any particular sect of Christians, in exclusion of all other Sects? That the same authority which can force a citizen to contribute three pence only of his property for the support of any one establishment, may force him to conform to any other establishment in all cases whatsoever?

The Bible-Reading Decision

In 1963, the year after the school prayer decision, the Supreme Court handed down its opinion in the case of *School District of Abington Township* v. *Schempp*, usually shortened as *Schempp*. The *Schempp* decision involved a Pennsylvania law that required the reading of at least ten verses from the Bible every day in public school. The readings from the Bible were to be followed by the Lord's Prayer and the Pledge of Allegiance.

The Pennsylvania law allowed all students whose parents requested exemption to be exempt from the readings and recitation. The Schempp family, however, challenged the law on the basis that certain Bible readings, if taken literally, were against their religious beliefs as Unitarians. The Schempps brought suit to stop the readings.

In an 8-to-1 decision, the Supreme Court declared that the Pennsylvania law requiring Bible readings in public school was unconstitutional.* Justice Tom Cark wrote the

---

*On the same day it handed down *Schempp*, the Court also handed down its decision in *Murray* v. *Curlett*. The *Murray* case involved a

opinion for the majority. "The place of religion in our society," he said, "is an exalted one, achieved through a long tradition of reliance on the home, the church and the inviolable citadel of the individual heart and mind."

But in America, Clark pointed out, the separation of church and state demands that the attitude government takes toward religion be *neutral.* "While protecting all, it prefers none, and it disparages none." The neutrality of government in religious affairs, he maintained, was "wholesome" because it permitted the development of religious pluralism. In the United States, every citizen had the right to pursue whatever religious training or belief he or she chose.

What test, Clark then asked, can be devised to determine if government has violated the neutrality it should show toward religious matters or if a law intrudes on the religious freedom guaranteed by the Constitution? The test, he maintained, is to ask ourselves what the "purpose and primary effect" of the law in question is. If the law acts to advance religion or inhibit it, then it exceeds the authority granted by the constitution. If it is neutral, then it is constitutionally acceptable.

With this test in mind, Clark turned to the Pennsylvania law requiring Bible reading. Pennsylvania claimed that its law did not "advance" religion, but benefited all public school children equally, regardless of their religious backgrounds. Among the benefits the students received, the state argued, were "the promotion of moral values, the contradiction to the materialistic trends of our times, the

---

challenge by Madelyn Murray and her son, both atheists, to a law requiring religious observances in public school. Because of the outspoken atheism of the mother, who became a nationally known figure, the *Murray* case received more notoriety than the *Schempp* decision.

perpetuation of our institutions and the teaching of literature."

Justice Clark regarded the Pennsylvania claims with suspicion. It may be, he acknowledged, that some of the benefits of the Bible-reading law were secular and nonreligious
and therefore acceptable. But at the same time, he pointed
out, the fact cannot be ignored that the benefits are "accomplished through readings, without comment," from a
book that is above all else a religious book. Readings from
any book that is primarily religious, like the Bible, Clark
concluded, amount to a religious exercise and cannot be
sanctioned by the state.

It was clear, Clark wrote, that Pennsylvania recognized
that the Bible-reading law raised religious problems. The
state had made attendance at the Bible readings voluntary,
and it permitted the substitution of the Catholic version of
the Bible for the Protestant wherever it was requested. If
the Bible-reading law had been truly neutral, Clark insisted, then the state would not have had to make these
exceptions. But the very fact that they had been made
showed that the state recognized that the law was controversial and could violate religious sensibilities.

Clark then turned to two final questions. Some Americans have argued, he wrote, that since a majority in the
United States favors religious exercises in public schools,
then the Court should bow to the will of that majority.
Still others, he added, have warned that unless religious
exercises are permitted, a "religion of secularism" will be
established in the schools that will undermine traditional
religious belief.

Clark discounted both arguments. The Supreme Court,
he claimed, cannot allow a state to require a religious exercise, even when a majority within that state consented to

such an exercise. The "free exercise of religion clause" in the Constitution, he insisted, "has never meant that a majority could use the machinery of the State to practice its beliefs" and thereby deny a minority the free exercise of its beliefs.

Nor does the Court's decision, Clark went on, undermine the practice of traditional religious faith. Nothing that has been said in the *Schempp* decision, he maintained, holds that "the study of the Bible or religion, when presented objectively as part of a secular program of education" would be unconstitutional. But the Bible readings, he added, do not fall into this secular category. "They are religious exercises" and are "required by the State in violation of the command of the First Amendment that the Government maintain strict neutrality, neither aiding nor opposing religion."

Dissent

Justice Potter Stewart was the only member of the Court to dissent in the public school prayer and Bible-reading decisions. In his dissent in the case involving school prayer, Stewart wrote, "The Court today decides that in permitting this brief nondenominational prayer the school board has violated the Constitution of the United States. I think this decision is wrong."

"With all respect," he continued, "I think the Court has misapplied a great constitutional principle. I cannot see how an 'official religion' is established by letting those who want to say a prayer say it." On the contrary, he claimed, "I think that to deny" the children who wish to say the prayer the opportunity to say it "is to deny them the opportunity of sharing in the spiritual heritage of our Nation."

The prayer, Stewart concluded, should be seen in a different way from that in which the majority of the court looked at it. It was not the establishment of a religion by the state of New York. What New York did in composing the prayer, he wrote, was "to recognize and to follow the deeply entrenched and highly cherished spiritual traditions" of America, traditions "which came down to us from those who almost two hundred years ago avowed their 'firm reliance on the Protection of Divine Providence' when they proclaimed the freedom and independence of this brave new world."

In his dissent in the Bible-reading case, Stewart pointed to two factors that bothered him. First, he noted that there was a "substantial free exercise claim" on the part of those parents who "affirmatively desire" to have their children's school day open with the reading of passages from the Bible. Since the Constitution provides for the "free exercise" of religion, he asked, should the Court be in the position of taking that right away? Shouldn't the parents who want the Bible readings be granted that privilege?

Second, Stewart argued that when the government "so structures a child's life" that religious exercises are not permitted in public schools, then the government has acted to place religion in a disadvantageous position. Viewed in this light, he concluded, "permission of such exercises for those who want them is necessary if the schools are truly to be neutral in the matter of religion."

The claims of the Court's majority, Stewart wrote, that neutrality had been attained in the *Schempp* decision were not accurate. The "refusal to permit religious activities" is not neutrality, he claimed. It is the establishment of a "religion of secularism." It is government endorsement of the beliefs of those who "think that religious exercises should be conducted only in private," and it is therefore unconstitutional because it amounts to the approval of one type of religious views over another.

Response to the Warren Court's Decisions on Religious Matters

Many American religious leaders voiced support for the Court's decisions on school prayer and Bible reading and emphasized the importance of the separation of church and state in America. Among them was Rabbi Albert Lewis of Los Angeles who declared after the Bible reading decision was handed down, "It is important that people not be misled by distorted statements about the decision. The Supreme Court has nowhere in its decision denied belief in God, prayer, religious songs, Bible reading, or any other religious belief or practice."

Other religious leaders, however, responded differently. Cardinal Spellman of New York was "shocked and frightened that the Supreme Court has declared unconstitutional a simple and voluntary declaration of belief in God by public school children." The decision, the cardinal maintained, "strikes at the very heart of the Godly tradition in which America's children have so long been raised."

Evangelist Billy Graham regarded the school prayer decision as "another step toward the secularization of the United States." In a phrase that was often quoted by the Court's critics, Graham argued that "the framers of our Constitution meant we were to have freedom *of* religion, not freedom *from* religion."

In a statement released after the Bible-reading decision, Graham claimed that 80 percent of the American people wanted Bible reading and prayer in public schools. "Why should the majority," he asked, "be so severely penalized by the protests of a handful?" Then, sounding a theme that was to become familiar in the protest over the Court's decisions, he said, "At a time when moral decadence is evident on every hand, when race tension is mounting, when the threat of Communism is growing, when terrifying new weapons of destruction are being created, we need more religion, not less."

Many in Congress agreed with Spellman and Graham. After the *Engel* decision striking down school prayer, Senator Sam Ervin (Democrat, North Carolina) declared "the Supreme Court has made God unconstitutional." The same decision provoked another southern Democrat, Herman Talmadge, to say that the members of the court had "never in the wildest of their excesses" gone as far as they had in declaring school prayer unconstitutional. This decision, he claimed, was an "alien" reading of the Constitution and was an attempt "to change our form of government."

Congressional opposition to the decision was expressed primarily through attempts to pass an amendment to the Constitution that would allow school prayer and Bible reading. The first such amendment was sponsored by Representative Frank Becker, a Republican from New York. The Becker amendment stated that nothing in the Constitution should be so construed as to prevent "the offering, reading from, or listening to prayer and biblical scriptures, if the participation therein is on a voluntary basis, in any government or public school institution or place."

Becker's amendment failed to reach the House floor for consideration and died in 1964. Two years later the Senate considered a similar bill sponsored by Senator Everett Dirksen. The Senate considered the Dirksen amendment, but failed to give it the necessary two-thirds vote for passage.

The movement in favor of school prayer and Bible reading, however, continued to gain momentum. In 1967 Representative Charlotte Reid (Democrat, Illinois) connected the country's growing crime rate and what she called widespread immorality and permissiveness with the abandonment of religious exercises in public schools. She joined the rapidly expanding number of people who believed that "traditional values" should be restored to the classroom.

In 1971, owing to pressure from a nationwide organization called the Prayer Campaign Committee, Congress once again considered a prayer amendment. This time, the amendment was sponsored by Chalmers Wylie, a Republican from Ohio. By September 1971 Wylie's petition in favor of the amendment had been signed by a majority in the House of Representatives and came up on the House floor for debate. On November 8 the amendment was approved by a vote of 240 to 162, but failed by 28 votes to receive the two-thirds vote necessary for passage.

At present the chances for the passage of a school prayer and Bible-reading amendment are greater than ever. Senator Jesse Helms, a conservative Republican from North Carolina and a highly influential politician, has made it part of his agenda for the nation. The Moral Majority and other fundamentalist and conservative religious groups strongly support its passage, and it has likewise received the endorsement of President Ronald Reagan.

The Warren Court's decisions involving freedom of religion demonstrate its strict approach to the rights guaranteed by the First Amendment. In considering the other rights mentioned in the First Amendment—freedom of

speech and the press, and the "right of the people peace-
ably to assemble"—the Warren Court was equally strict and
absolutist.

Thus the Warren court struck down laws designed against
Communists and other "subversive" groups, because these
laws restricted freedom of expression. The Court likewise
struck down traditional laws regarding pornography and
obscenity. It declared that there were indeed such things
as pornography and obscenity, but failed to come up with a
workable definition that could be used to ban the pornographic and the obscene.

All these decisions aroused great controversy. Critics
continued to charge that the Court had claimed too much
power to itself. Defenders of the Warren Court lauded the
Court for its strong defense of individual freedom and liberty. Never, they claimed, had the Court done so much for
the poor, for the powerless, and for minority groups, as it
had done under Warren.

CHAPTER SEVEN
Postscript on the Warren Court

> In recent years the Court has woven about the Constitution
> a cloak of political theory to protect and promote human
> dignity—Comment on the Warren Court by constitutional
> scholar A. T. Mason.

During the 1930s the noted constitutional scholar E. S.
Corwin predicted that the Supreme Court of the future
would have plenty to do if it intervened "on behalf of the
helpless and oppressed." The high court, he added, would
then "be free, as it has not in many years, to support the
humane values of free thought, free utterance, and fair
play." He believed that the Supreme Court of the future
would be able "to give voice to the conscience of the country" and play a new role in constitutional history.

The Warren Court carried out Professor Corwin's predic-
tions. On behalf of the "oppressed" and "helpless," the
Warren revolution instituted changes in race relations, political apportionment, and the rights of the accused. For
Chief Justice Warren, the provisions of the Bill of Rights
constituted "the heart of any constitution" and it was the
Court's "judicial duty and responsibility" to see that these
rights were made available to all Americans. Reporters and
political commentators called the Warren Court decisions
"myth-shattering" and "precedent-breaking."

A few statistics reveal the change that came in the Supreme Court under the leadership of Earl Warren. In the 1935–36 term the Hughes Court handed down 160 decisions with written opinions. Only two of the 160 decisions involved questions of civil rights and civil liberties. In the 1960–61 term, the seventh under Warren, the Court handed down 120 decisions with opinions, of which 54 involved civil rights and liberties. In twenty-five years the focus of the Court's interest had altered drastically.

A. T. Mason, professor emeritus of jurisprudence at Princeton University, has compared the Warren Court with the Court under Chief Justice John Marshall. Under both chief justices, Mason argues, the Supreme Court became "a creative force in American life" and played a dynamic and positive role in the improvement of American society. John Marshall and Earl Warren, he concludes, were the two great activist chief justices in American judicial history.

Another constitutional scholar, Robert Steamer, agrees. In his book, *The Supreme Court in Crisis,* Steamer contends that the Warren Court played a historic role in the spread of the *substance* of democracy rather than its form or shell. The two great themes of the Warren Court, he adds, were "fairness" and "equality," and it was these two themes the Court attempted to make a living and real part of American life. Steamer recognizes the irony that the Supreme Court, regarded as the least democratic branch of government, should have been at the forefront of democratic change in the 1950s and 1960s.

As Steamer goes on to point out, however, the Warren Court's notions of "fairness" and "equality" are ideals that will inevitably "shake the establishment and the vested" interests in any society where they are put into practice.

They will arouse antagonism and bitter resentment, and they will be regarded as destructive and dangerous. New ideas of constitutional practice, like those adopted by the Warren Court, will be attacked and challenged by those who abhor rapid change or a marked break with the practices of the past.

The depth of the controversy aroused by the Warren Court revealed the scale and degree of the changes it was making in judicial practice. Beginning with its 1954 *Brown* decision, the Warren Court provoked a nationwide debate over the role of the Supreme Court in the American system of government, an argument that has not yet come to an end. The debate had its roots in the past, but was renewed with unusual fervor and commitment after 1954.

In 1958 the chief justices of the forty-eight states voted 36 to 8 to condemn the judicial activism of the Warren Court. Four chief justices abstained. The chief justices likewise denounced what they found to be the hastily written and ill-considered opinions of the Warren Court and attacked the Court for carrying on its work "without proper judicial restraint."

One of the most articulate and widely respected critics of the Warren Court's activities and decisions sat on the Court—Justice John Marshall Harlan. Many of the Court's most controversial decisions, Harlan claimed, reflected nothing but "a piece of ideology" or a "political theory" and amounted to "hazardous experimentation."

The Court, he believed, must not adopt one interpretation of the Constitution to the exclusion of all other interpretations:

•   •   •

However, it is all wrong, in my view, for the Court to adopt the political doctrines popularly accepted at the particular moment of our history and to declare all others to be irrational and invidious, barring them from the range of choice by reasonably minded people acting through the political process.

The Warren Court's belief that the Constitution rigidly imposed "upon Americans an ideology of unrestrained egalitarianism," he declared, was nothing but a "judicial creation" that could not withstand legal analysis.

Harlan challenged the ideology of the Warren Court in two speeches in the early 1960s. The Warren Court's ardent defense of the Bill of Rights, he declared before the American Bar Center in Chicago on August 13, 1963, has been at the expense of the federal principle and the separation of powers between the states and the nation. And the values of federalism, he added, "lie at the root of our constitutional system."

The next year, Harlan further discussed his fears for the future of federalism in a speech in New York City. "We are accustomed," he said, "to speak of the Bill of Rights and the Fourteenth Amendment as the principal guarantees of personal liberty." But we must also recognize, he warned, that our free society equally depends on the "structure of our political system." The Founding Fathers "staked their faith that liberty would prosper in the new nation," but they did so, Harlan claimed, not because of the guarantees they included in the Bill of Rights. Rather, they believed that freedom would flow primarily from the *kind* of government the Union would have.

It was the *kind* of government and its *structure* that Harlan believed the Warren Court had altered. By assuming too much power, the Court had altered the traditional and constitutional balance between the judiciary and the other two branches of the federal government. But, more significantly, it had altered the relationship between the federal government and the states.

Because the Court had imposed nationwide standards, derived from the Bill of Rights, on all the states, the states were no longer free to experiment and innovate in new directions based on their own traditions and needs. The state governments, Harlan feared, were now left with little to do but carry out dictates handed down from the Supreme Court and the federal judiciary.

In April 1965 Justice Arthur Goldberg answered some of the criticism that had been leveled by Harlan and others. Goldberg expressed his comments in a decision he wrote for the Court. He admitted that it was "one of the happy incidents of the federal system" that a state could serve as a laboratory and "try novel social and economic experiments," without harassment from the federal judiciary. But the right to try different social experiments, he went on, should not include "the power to experiment with the fundamental liberties of citizens safeguarded by the Bill of Rights."

Goldberg maintained that Harlan's notion of judicial restraint did nothing to advance the interests of the states or improve federalism. When the Supreme Court denies a state the right to "impair a fundamental constitutional right," he wrote, it does not thereby increase the power of the federal government at the expense of the state. On the contrary, the powers of both the state and the federal government are limited "in favor of safeguarding the fundamental rights and liberties of the individual."

Goldberg made one defense of the activist Warren Court. The constitutional scholar A. T. Mason has made another. The Warren Court, Mason argues in an essay entitled "Understanding the Warren Court," "quickened" the "social conscience" of America and helped to make "vocal and audible ideals that might otherwise be silenced." The Warren Court helped to make change possible where it had once been impossible.

This, Mason writes, is especially true in regard to the Court's decisions involving race relations and reapportionment. In these instances, he points out, minorities that once were "helpless in the face of a majority . . . bent on curbing their freedom" now have a voice in government. In making its drive for greater equality and fairness under the law, the Warren Court asserted its "special responsibility toward moral and spiritual values that lie at the base of our culture."

By opening American society up, Mason continues, and by giving ever larger numbers of people a role to play in the political system, the Warren Court made change possible without recourse to violent revolution. By offering hope that bad or unjust laws could be changed through the judicial system, the Court helped offset the belief that meaningful improvement could come only through violence against the established order.

The Warren Court, Mason maintains, revealed the special genius of the *independent* judiciary in the American system. This special genius, he explains, is the ability of the Court to interpose "courageously . . . its judgment against majorities bent on infractions of the Constitution" thereby protecting the rights of minorities and advancing the cause of peaceable change.

The Warren Court, Mason concludes, by "expanding the

limits of freedom" but at the same time "buttressing the moral foundations of society" and "keeping open constitutional alternatives to violent change," has brought us "closer to the ideals we have long professed" as a nation.

PART TWO

The Burger Court: Transition to Judicial Conservatism

When an old Court is suddenly reconstituted there will be unsettlement until the new judges have taken their positions on constitutional doctrine. During that time—which may extend a decade or two—constitutional law will be in flux. That is the necessary consequence of our system—Justice William O. Douglas.

CHAPTER EIGHT
The Crisis of Transition

We are very quiet here, but it is the quiet of a hurricane—
Justice Oliver Wendell Holmes (1841–1935), describing the
character of the Supreme Court.

On June 26, 1968, President Lyndon Johnson announced
that Chief Justice Earl Warren intended to resign. This in
itself was unusual. Warren, though seventy-seven, was still
vigorous, and most of the thirteen chief justices who pre-
ceded him had died in office. The announcement of the
intended resignation, however, set off a series of events
that were unprecedented in Supreme Court history.

First, Congress refused to consider the man Johnson
chose to replace Chief Justice Warren. Then, for the first
time, an associate justice resigned under charges of misuse
of office and corruption. Following that, two presidential
nominations to the high court were rejected in succession,
after a bitter and acrimonious fight in the Senate. Finally,
impeachment proceedings were begun in the House of
Representatives against yet another member of the Court.

These events resulted from the struggle to shape the
character of the future Court. Conservatives, on the one
hand, saw the resignation of the chief justice, the symbol of
liberalism and activism, as a chance to turn the Court around,
an opportunity to challenge and perhaps overrule the decisions of the Warren era. Liberals, on the other hand,

wanted to maintain a liberal Court. In the end, the conservatives won, but not without a battle that left representatives of both sides angry and resentful.

Chief Justice Warren Resigns

The day after he announced that Chief Justice Warren intended to resign, President Johnson announced his appointment of Abe Fortas to the chief justiceship. Fortas was already on the Court; three years earlier Johnson had named him an associate justice to replace Arthur Goldberg, who retired to become the ambassador to the United Nations. To take the seat on the Court that Fortas would vacate, Johnson appointed Congressman Homer Thornberry, a Democrat from Texas.

At first, the Fortas nomination seemed safe. The Senate has customarily approved a President's selection for chief justice without much ado. Most observers believed that Fortas would win his seat after a brief struggle. The nominee, who had just turned fifty-eight, would have many years to lead the Court and continue the policies of Chief Justice Warren.

But this was the problem. Several conservative senators rankled at the nomination of the liberal, activist Fortas. President Johnson, they pointed out, was a "lameduck" President. He had already announced that he would not be a candidate for reelection in the fall campaign. Why should he, they asked, have the opportunity to name a man who might head the Court for the next two or three decades?

Moreover, the Republicans believed that they would put a man of their own in the White House after the November elections. There was widespread dissatisfaction with the policies of the Democrats under President Johnson. The country was turning against the Vietnam War and was weary of the racial unrest and student radicalism that were characteristic of the late 1960s. And if a Republican nominee won, he would be certain to nominate a conservative to head the Court.

The Republican senators who opposed Fortas were led by Robert Griffin of Michigan. Looking for an issue on which to defeat the nomination, they first accused the President of cronyism—appointing close personal friends to high office. The charge, however, was a weak one, as Senator Dirksen, the Senate Republican leader, pointed out. You shouldn't expect, Dirksen said, the President to appoint his enemies to office.

The opponents of the nomination then charged that Fortas, while serving as an associate justice, had participated in White House conferences and in strategy sessions on the Vietnam War. These, they claimed were questionable activities for a member of the Court, because in the American system of government the judiciary and executive branches are supposed to remain separate. Fortas replied to the charges by pointing out, correctly, that many Supreme Court justices in the past had acted as advisers to Presidents.

Nevertheless, there was so much dissatisfaction with the nomination that the Senate Judiciary Committee decided to hold hearings on Fortas. It was the first time the committee had ever held hearings on a man named to the chief justiceship. Fortas was questioned severely. The senators did not ask him questions about his decisions on the Court; to have done so would have been a violation of the separation of powers. But they did read to him from liberal opinions he had written in a manner that revealed their disagreement.

The Judiciary Committee approved the nomination 17 to

6, but when the nomination came up for a Senate vote, it ran into trouble. A new charge against Fortas appeared: that he had accepted a $15,000 fee for a series of lectures. The fee had been paid by a wealthy businessman, a friend of Fortas's former law partner, who might have cases coming before the Court.

Conservative Republican and Democratic senators decided to stage a filibuster—long speeches intended to prevent a vote being taken—in order to block the nomination. In an emotional speech, Senator Dirksen, who had previously supported Fortas, turned against him. What had changed his mind, Dirksen explained, was that the Warren Court had just overturned a sentence of death imposed on the murderer of a Chicago policeman. What the Court needed, he added, was fewer liberal justices and more who favored law and order.

The filibuster was successful. For four days, the Senate debated the nomination, and then voted to cut off debate. The vote, 45 to 43, was fourteen votes short of the two-thirds necessary to end the filibuster under Senate rules. Two days later, Fortas withdrew his name from consideration. It was the first time in Senate history that a filibuster had blocked the nomination of a chief justice to the Supreme Court.

Chief Justice Warren stayed on the Court another year and then submitted his resignation to President Richard Nixon. To replace Warren, Nixon submitted the name of Warren Burger to the Senate. On June 9, 1969, the Senate approved the nomination by a vote of 74 to 3. Burger had served on the Court of Appeals for the District of Columbia for fourteen years and a reputation as a moderate to conservative judge. Burger was Nixon's first nomination to the

Court and his first step toward reshaping the Warren tradition.

The Crisis Continues

The withdrawal of his name from consideration for the office of Chief Justice did not end the controversy surrounding Abe Fortas. In May 1969 *Life* magazine carried an article which revealed that Fortas had accepted another high fee from a questionable source. The fee was a $20,000 yearly grant from the family foundation of Louis Wolfsen. Wolfsen had been convicted for selling unregistered stock and was, at the time the article appeared, in prison.

Fortas had received only one $20,000 gift from the Wolfsen Foundation and had returned the money once he learned about Wolfsen's reputation and realized the impropriety of accepting the gift. But the revelation had permanently damaged his reputation. When rumors of similar indiscretions on his part began to gain wide currency, he resigned from the Court on May 16, 1969, and returned to private practice.

The Fortas resignation gave Nixon a second, and unexpected, opportunity to appoint a justice early in his first term. Declaring his firm belief in the importance of a "strict interpretation" of the Constitution, the President nominated Clement Haynesworth to replace the discredited Fortas. Haynesworth, from South Carolina, was chief judge of the U. S. Circuit Court of Appeals for the Fourth Circuit.

The nomination set off a bitter controversy. The AFL-CIO and other labor organizations charged that many of Haynesworth's decisions on the Circuit Court had been antilabor and antiworker. The NAACP charged the appointee with racism and antiblack feelings, because he had taken restrictive views on desegregation cases.

These attacks alone would not have been sufficient to block Haynesworth from the Court, but then liberal Senator Birch Bayh (Democrat, Indiana) found evidence that Judge Haynesworth had ruled in favor of firms in which he held stock. Such activities might not be strictly illegal, Haynesworth's critics charged, but they did reveal a gross insensitivity toward judicial ethics. It would have been proper, they asserted, for the judge to withdraw from decisions that involved his own finances.

Fortas had been brought low by revelations of judicial misconduct and so would Haynesworth. Seventeen Senate Republicans, including Hugh Scott of Pennsylvania, the minority leader, joined the Democrats in rejecting Haynesworth by a vote of 55 to 45. An angry President Nixon charged that the attacks on his nominee had been "brutal, vicious, and . . . unfair," but vowed to continue his search for a conservative to sit on the Court.

In his second attempt to find a replacement for Fortas, Nixon named G. Harold Carswell to the Court. Carswell, who was from Florida, had served for seven years as a federal district judge and for the past six months had been on the U. S. Court of Appeals. He had a moderately conservative reputation.

Most senators did not want a repetition of the bitter struggle over the nomination of Haynesworth and, at first, Carswell's prospects looked good. But it soon became clear that Carswell had problems. A reporter discovered that Carswell in a 1948 speech had made racist statements. "Segregation of the races is proper and the only practical and correct way of life in our states," he had said.

When asked about the statement, Carswell claimed that he no longer held those beliefs and now found them "obnoxious and abhorrent." But new revelations found that he presently belonged to an all-white club in Tallahassee and had participated actively in the club's efforts to keep blacks out. Furthermore, he had on more than one occasion insulted civil rights lawyers in his court. The NAACP came out firmly against the nomination.

Carswell was also charged with mediocrity. His decisions as a lower federal judge were frequently reversed in higher courts, and his judicial work, his critics said, was without distinction. Senator Roman Hruska (Republican, Nebraska) attempted to defend Carswell in a television interview. "Even if he were mediocre," Hruska said, "there are a lot of mediocre judges and people and lawyers. Aren't they entitled to a little representation and a little chance?" But Hruska's appeal fell flat. No one wanted a mediocre judicial talent on the Court.

By a vote of 13 to 4, Carswell received the approval of the Judiciary Committee. The approval of his nomination still seemed likely. On the Senate floor, however, his opponents were able to postpone consideration of his name until after the Easter recess. This allowed them time to lobby against Carswell and to convince uncertain senators that he should not be allowed on the Court.

Concerned about the fate of his nominee, President Nixon wrote a letter to Senator William Saxbe (Republican, Ohio). In the letter, Nixon claimed that he was "the one person entrusted by the Constitution with the power of appointment." The Senate had the power of advice and consent on nominations, the President acknowledged, but this power was a mere "formality." If the Senate attempts to substitute its judgment as to who should be appointed, he concluded, "the traditional constitutional balance is in jeopardy and the duty of the President under the Constitution is impaired."

The Senate did not accept the President's argument. Under the Constitution it, too, had the power to shape and mold the Supreme Court, a power it did not want to relinquish. On April 8, 1970, the vote on Carswell came to the Senate floor. The nomination was defeated by a vote of 45 to 51. Once again, many prominent Senate Republicans voted against their President's nominee.

And once again the President was angered. "With the Senate as presently constituted," he said, "I cannot successfully nominate to the Supreme Court any federal appellate judge from the South who believes as I do in the strict construction of the Constitution. Judges Carswell and Haynesworth have endured with admirable dignity vicious assaults on their intelligence, their honesty, and their character.

"When all the hypocrisy is stripped away," the President continued, the real reason for the failure of the nominations became obvious. Haynesworth and Carswell were conservative in their judicial philosophy, he added, "a philosophy that I share." It was this philosophy that led to their defeat, not the charges of misdeeds or mediocrity, he concluded.

Six days after the Carswell defeat in the Senate, Nixon appointed Harry Blackmun to the post vacated by Fortas. Blackmun, from Minnesota, was a federal appeals court judge, widely respected for his scholarly and thorough opinions. Although he was regarded as a moderate conservative, his nomination readily passed the Senate by a vote of 94 to 0.

President Nixon had experienced the defeat of two successive nominations to the Supreme Court, and the defeats rankled. In the twentieth century only one other President, Herbert Hoover, had had a nominee to the Court turned down. That was in 1930, more than forty years earlier. As a result of the long struggle to replace Fortas, the Court functioned for the 1969–70 term without a full complement of nine justices, the first time a seat had been left vacant for so long a time since the Civil War.

A Question of Impeachment

The struggle to reshape the Supreme Court continued. Supporters of Haynesworth and Carswell in Congress decided to begin impeachment proceedings against the man who was for them the symbol of Supreme Court liberalism: Justice William O. Douglas. If Douglas was discredited and forced to resign or was impeached, another liberal seat on the Court would be vacant.

Vice-President Spiro Agnew joined the attack. It was time, Agnew said, to take a "good look" at Justice Douglas. "At the present time," he explained, "all I'm advocating is that Justice Douglas's record be thoroughly examined, including his writings and his verbal opinions, to see whether they are compatible with the position he holds" on the Supreme Court.

Rumors of impeachment were not new to Douglas. In 1953, after he had voted for a stay of execution for Julius and Ethel Rosenberg, who had been convicted of espionage for the Soviet Union, there had been a clamor for his removal from office. Justice Douglas had likewise been frequently denounced for his unconventional life-style, which had included four wives, three divorces, and a remarriage in 1966 at the age of sixty-seven to a woman of twenty-three. But Douglas and his friends regarded the 1970 impeachment proceedings as more serious than the earlier attacks.

The first step in the impeachment proceedings came on April 15 and was made by Representative Gerald Ford of Michigan, a leading House Republican who was later to replace the Vice-President, after Agnew left office in disgrace, and then become President upon the resignation of Richard Nixon. In a speech before the House of Representatives, Ford asked what an impeachable offense was and then proceeded to answer his question.

An impeachable offense, he declared, "is whatever a majority of the House of Representatives considers to be at a given moment in history." And conviction, he continued, "results from whatever offense or offenses two-thirds of the [Senate] considers to be sufficiently serious to require removal of the accused from office." An impeachable offense, then, was whatever the Congress said it was, because there were few "fixed principles" from among the "handful of precedents" to make a judgment on.

In considering impeachable offenses, however, Ford maintained that "a higher standard is expected of federal judges than of any other 'civil officers' of the United States." Federal judges, he implied, could be impeached for behavior that might be tolerated in lesser officials. With this in mind, he concluded, "let us now objectively examine certain aspects of the behavior of Mr. Justice Douglas, and let us ask ourselves" if this behavior represents what we want and respect in our judges.

Ford then went on to list what he believed to be several of Douglas's violations of high judicial standards. First, Ford pointed to a recent article by Douglas, a prolific author, in *Avant Garde*, a New York magazine. Douglas, he said, had "reportedly" accepted payment for the article. Ford found this questionable because the publisher of *Avant Garde*, Ralph Ginzburg, had twice, once in 1966 and again in 1970, been involved in cases before the Supreme Court. In both cases, the Court had decided against Ginzburg, but Douglas had dissented in Ginzburg's favor. Ford wondered if Douglas should have published in Ginzburg's magazine. Did the acceptance of money for the article represent a conflict of interest?

Ford then called into question the propriety of a Supreme Court justice publishing anything in a magazine like *Avant Garde*. The publisher of the magazine, Ford said, was disreputable. He had twice been convicted for the publication of obscene material and had successfully been sued for libel after he had published in his earlier magazine, *Fact*, a scurrilous attack on Senator Barry Goldwater. Was this the sort of publisher, Ford asked, who should publish works by a high official in American government?

Ford went on to attack Justice Douglas's most recent book, *Points of Rebellion* (1970). The book, Ford suggested, supported radical attacks on American society and inspired a lack of respect for American traditions. Moreover, Ford added, Douglas had allowed sections of his book to be published in the *Evergreen Review* right next to pictures that could only be considered pornographic.

Ford's final criticism of Justice Douglas centered on the justice's association with the Parvin Foundation, from which Douglas received a $12,000 a year honorarium. Ford linked Parvin and his foundation to "known gambling figures and Mafia types." He declared that this made the justice a "well-paid moonlighter for an organization whose ties to the international gambling fraternity have never been sufficiently explored." To shore up his accusation, Ford used unconfirmed material that had been supplied to him by Attorney General John Mitchell and had come from FBI and CIA files.

More than one hundred conservative representatives, both Democrats and Republicans, called for an investigation of the charges against Justice Douglas. The responsibility for the investigation was given to the House Judiciary Committee. Emanuel Celler (Democrat, New York), the chairman of the committee, appointed a select subcommittee to look into the charges and determine if impeachment of Douglas should be carried out.

Justice Douglas denied the charges that had been made against him. He believed that he had the right to be published wherever he pleased and said that at no time had he accepted payment that represented a conflict of interest. His duties for the Parvin Foundation, he explained, amounted to a membership on a committee that helped select impoverished foreign students from Third World countries for scholarships to study in the United States.

In May, a month after they had been launched, the impeachment proceedings against Douglas came to a stop. In their book, *The Brethren** (1979), reporters Bob Woodward and Scott Armstrong revealed the reasons behind the sudden shift. President Nixon, they claim, had come to the conclusion that the impeachment of Douglas was not a good idea. The evidence against the justice was thin and insubstantial. Moreover, Chief Justice Burger had indicated that the attack on the senior member of the Supreme Court was

*The title of *The Brethren* comes from the practice Supreme Court justices have of referring to fellow justices as "Brother Burger" or "Brother Douglas." Collectively, therefore, in the past the Court could be referred to as "the Brethren."

bad for the Court as a whole and undermined respect for the judiciary.

According to Woodward and Armstrong, Nixon informed Attorney General Mitchell that the attack should be called off. Mitchell, in response, drafted a speech to be made before the bar association of the District of Columbia. In the speech, the attorney general condemned the "irresponsible and malicious" criticism of the Supreme Court and demanded that the criticism be brought to an end. Opponents of Douglas in Congress got the message and stopped the impeachment proceedings.

Justice Douglas gives another account of the end of the proceedings in the second volume of his autobiography, *The Court Years* (1980). According to Douglas, his old friend, Irving Brant, without Douglas's urging, sent a paper to the House Judiciary Committee arguing that impeachment, according to the Constitution, could be justified only "for conviction of treason, bribery, or other high crimes and misdemeaners." Since it was clear that Douglas could not be charged with any wrongdoing of this caliber, the committee abandoned the task and issued reports that simply listed the charges against the justice as "without substance."

The New Court

Despite the bitter controversy that arose during the last year of the Warren Court and continued through the first year of the Burger Court, President Nixon was able to reshape and remold the Court. His first appointment was Chief Justice Burger, a conservative. His second was the moderately conservative Harry Blackmun. Before his resignation in 1974, Nixon was able to make two further appointments to the high court.

In September 1971 Justice Hugo Black and Justice John Harlan retired from the Court within a few days of one another. Black, eighty-four, had served thirty-four years as a justice and was known as the Court's most ardent defender of the Bill of Rights. Harlan, seventy-two, had served for sixteen years and was a champion of judicial restraint. The two justices were nevertheless warm personal friends.

President Nixon now had the opportunity to appoint two new justices at the same time, an opportunity last enjoyed by President Roosevelt in 1940. To replace Justice Black, Nixon turned to Lewis Powell, a southerner and a man of outstanding qualifications. Powell was a sixty-four-year-old attorney in private practice in Richmond, Virginia, and a past president of the American Bar Association. As a member of the Richmond school board in the 1950s, he urged that the city's schools remain open throughout the program of "massive resistance" to desegregation.

For Harlan's seat, Nixon chose William Rehnquist, a native of Arizona. Rehnquist, forty-seven, had already made a name for himself as a brilliant defender of conservative causes. At the time of his nomination, he was serving in the Nixon administration as an assistant attorney general. Rehnquist was to become the youngest member of the Burger Court, as well as its most conservative.

Nixon announced the nominations of Powell and Rehnquist on October 21, 1971. Powell had no problem in the Senate and was readily approved on December 6, by a vote of 89 to 1. Rehnquist faired less well. It was discovered that in 1952 he had written a memorandum for Justice Robert Jackson, whom he served as law clerk.

The memorandum defended segregation and spoke

favorably about the separation of whites and blacks. The Senate Judiciary Committee challenged him on the memorandum, but Rehnquist explained that its views were not his and had not been his at the time it was written. He had merely been expressing the views of the justice he served. On December 10, 1971, he was confirmed by a vote of 68 to 26.

The Burger Court now held four new justices; five remained from the Warren years. But with the retirement of Justice Douglas in November 1975, the Burger Court had its new majority. In January of that year Douglas had suffered a stroke that severely incapacitated him, but he had attempted to carry on his work. It soon became evident, however, that his illness prevented him from assuming a full work load, and he announced his resignation.

President Ford chose John Paul Stevens of Chicago to replace Douglas, who had served longer on the Supreme Court than any other justice in history, thirty-six years and seven months. Stevens was a judge in the U. S. Court of Appeals for the Seventh Circuit, a jurist with a reputation for scholarly and well-written opinions. He was a moderate Republican, more a "centrist" than a conservative.

The Supreme Court now held two conservatives—Chief Justice Burger and Justice Rehnquist—and three moderately conservative men, Justices Powell, Blackmun, and Stevens. Of the four Warren Court members who remained, only two were regarded as liberals, Justices William Brennan and Thurgood Marshall.* The other two, Stewart and White, were moderates.

---

*Marshall was appointed to the Court by President Johnson in 1968 to replace Justice Clark, who retired. In Chapter Two, we saw that Marshall had been a highly successful civil rights lawyer, arguing many cases

Only two of the nine Burger Court justices had been appointed by Democratic Presidents. The remaining seven had been the choice of Republicans. Ten years earlier the Warren Court had held a majority of justices appointed by Democratic administrations. The struggle to reorient the Court had been successful. In the next chapters, however, we shall see that the Court was to move very slowly in the direction President Nixon hoped it would move and that it has yet to become the Court of a conservative's dreams.

---

before the high court, including *Brown* v. *Board of Education*. He was the Supreme Court's first black justice.

The Warren Court in 1955. Center, front row: Chief Justice Earl Warren; left to right, front row: Associate Justices Felix Frankfurter, Hugo Black (Warren), Stanley Reed, William Douglas; back row: Associate Justices Sherman Minton, Harold Burton, Tom Clark, John Harlan.

Wide World Photos

Clarence Earl Gideon, whose appeal to the Supreme Court brought the decision in 1962 that expanded the right to counsel to cover cases in state courts.

Wide World Photos

The Burger Court. Center, front row: Chief Justice Warren Burger; left to right, front row: Associate Justices Byron White, William Brennan (Burger), Potter Stewart, Thurgood Marshall; back row: Associate Justices William Rehnquist, Henry Blackmun, Lewis Powell, John Paul Stevens.

United States Supreme Court

A participant in a demonstration on abortion talking with reporters outside the Supreme Court building in Washington. *Wide World Photos*

A group demonstrating in protest of the Supreme Court's decision in the Bakke case in 1978. *Wide World Photos*

Sandra Day O'Connor is sworn in as an Associate Justice of the Supreme Court by the Chief Justice as Mrs. O'Connor's husband holds the Bibles. *Michael Evans, The White House*

CHAPTER NINE
The Burger Court and the Rights of Criminals

> Today we have the most complicated system of criminal justice and the most difficult system to administer of any country in the world. To a large extent this is the result of judicial decisions which in effect made drastic revisions of the code of criminal procedure and evidence, and to a substantial extent imposed these procedures on the states—
> From a Columbus, Ohio, speech of Warren Burger in 1968, the year before he became chief justice.

Many conservative Americans hoped that the Burger Court would move quickly to establish a new judicial philosophy for the federal court system. Since the chief pillars of the Warren revolution had been the rights of criminals, race relations, and reapportionment, conservatives watched these areas closely. Would the Burger Court be able to overrule precedents established by the Warren Court? Would the new chief justice retreat from judicial activism and return to judicial restraint?

Few of the Warren Court's decisions had been more controversial than the decisions involving criminal rights. Throughout the country, numerous people and groups urged that the Court abandon what they regarded as its extreme opinions in the *Escobedo* and *Miranda* cases. Among the more prominent of these critics was Warren Burger, the new chief justice. Would Burger, now that he stood at the head of the Supreme Court, be able to make his views a part of the law of the land?

The Opinions of the New Chief Justice

During the year before he was nominated to the high court, Burger made two speeches on the criminal justice system. The speeches, which were critical of the Warren Court, so impressed President Nixon that he chose Burger to be chief justice and to be the man to turn the Court around.

Burger delivered his first speech in Columbus, Ohio, on September 4, 1968. "As we look back," he began, "we can see that for about the first one hundred fifty years of our history, the criminal law and its procedures remained fairly simple and quite stable." But "for twenty-five to thirty years after that there was considerable ferment in criminal procedure and the rules of evidence, and in the last ten years [the years of the Warren Courty we have witnessed what many scholars describe as a 'revolution in criminal law.'"

Some of these revolutionary changes, Burger claimed, "were long overdue." American lawyers, he believed, should take pride "in a case like *Gideon* v. *Wainwright*," which guarantees a lawyer to every person charged with a serious offense. Likewise, Burger went on, the Court's decisions "on right to counsel . . . and on coerced confession will always be regarded as landmarks on basic rights."

All of those decisions, Burger said, "were appropriate subjects for definitive constitutional holdings," even though "some states had achieved these improvements long before the Supreme Court did so." Burger then turned directly to his disagreement with the Warren Court. Where the War-

ren Court went wrong, he maintained, was in the changes
it made in the rules that guide criminal law.

Thirty years ago, Burger pointed out, Congress established an advisory committee to accomplish the "comprehensive" and "enormous" task of overseeing criminal
justice. Burger admitted that the process established by
Congress was slow, but added that he believed it was the
"tested" and orderly means to accomplish changes in criminal law.

But instead of allowing this process to work, the Warren
Court had opted to follow its own method of revising criminal justice, and it was this method that aroused widespread
controversy. "It seems clear now," Burger concluded, "that
the Supreme Court should have used the mechanism provided by Congress for making rules of criminal procedure
rather than changing the criminal procedure and rules of
evidence on a case-by-case basis."

Six months later, on March 14, 1969, Burger made a
speech at Ripon College where he addressed more directly
the frustrations many Americans felt over the present criminal justice system. "Is a society which frequently takes five
to ten years to dispose of a single criminal case," he asked,
"entitled to call itself an 'organized' society? . . . Is a judicial system, which consistently finds it necessary to try a
criminal case three, four or five times deserving of the
confidence and respect of decent people?"

Burger answered these questions with a resounding no.
Criminal justice in the United States, he believed, was
tilted toward the criminal rather than toward the victim
and the needs of society. Other liberal, freedom-loving
Western democracies—like the Netherlands, Sweden, and
Denmark—he pointed out, have far simpler, more effi-

cient, and speedier systems of criminal justice, yet they do not sacrifice the rights of their citizens.

Moreover, Burger added, these nations have better prisons, where emphasis is placed on rehabilitation of the criminal. These societies do not regard the criminal as "human rubbish" once the trial is over, as America has tended to do. In Sweden, Burger concluded, where justice is more efficient and speedier than it is in the United States, the murder rate is only 4 percent of what it is in the United States.

Thus Burger's vision of an improved criminal justice system rested on two notions. First, the Court need not hamper the states by imposing rules that must be followed nationwide. Changes in criminal justice come best through agencies other than the Supreme Court. Second, if the Court is going to play a role in improving criminal procedure it should be by making the system more efficient and speedier. The duty of the Court is to make the system less difficult to administer, not more.

The Burger Court Looks at Criminal Procedure

In his vigorous dissent to the controversial *Miranda* decision, Justice John Harlan had observed: "This Court is forever adding new stories to the temples of constitutional law, and the temples have a way of collapsing when one story too many is added." His prediction proved true. During the 1970s the Burger Court began chipping away at the "one story too many" it believed the Warren Court had added to the practice of criminal law.

The most widely denounced criminal law decisions of the Warren years were *Escobedo* and *Miranda*. In those two cases the Court had developed its notion that defendants must be warned of their right to remain silent and to have a lawyer as soon as they become suspects in a crime. The two cases likewise extended the exclusionary rule: any statements defendants they made before they were warned of their rights had to be excluded as evidence in their trials.

One of the first opportunities the Burger Court had to address this doctrine came in the case of *Harris* v. *New York* in 1971. The case involved an individual who was arrested for a crime and then tried. During his trial, he took the stand and made statements that conflicted with statements he had made to the police before he was warned of his rights. His earlier testimony to the police was revived and used against him. He was convicted and sent to prison.

From prison Harris sued, claiming that the evidence used against him had been obtained illegally. His case rose through the federal courts and came to the Supreme Court. One of the questions before the high court was whether the *Miranda* warnings were absolute and applied in every case or whether qualifications could be made in the *Miranda* precedent.

In a 5-to-4 decision, the Burger Court qualified the *Miranda* precedent. The Court agreed that statements made by a defendant before he was advised of his rights could not be used against him in a trial. But these statements could be used to impeach his credibility as a witness, if he took the stand in his own defense and made statements that conflicted with those he had made earlier.

Chief Justice Burger wrote the opinion for the majority. "It does not follow from *Miranda*," Burger argued, "that evidence inadmissible against an accused . . . is barred for all purposes," provided that the evidence satisfies legal standards. The *Miranda* requirements, he concluded, cannot be allowed to let a defendant lie on the stand, if trustworthy evidence shows that he is lying.

The *Harris* decision qualified *Miranda* by allowing evidence to be submitted in a trial that the Warren Court would probably have barred. Other qualifications of Warren Court decisions were to follow:

• In 1972 Justice Rehnquist deliverd a majority opinion which declared that a tip from a reliable informer allowed police forcibly to stop a suspect, search the suspect and his car, and reach for the spot where the informer had told them a gun was hidden.

• In 1973 the Burger Court upheld two convictions, one a traffic violation, the other a charge of narcotics possession. In both cases, the defendants protested that the police had violated their Fourth Amendment rights by conducting "unreasonable searches and seizures."

The Court upheld the convictions, arguing that the police did not need "additional justification" to conduct searches for further incriminating evidence after making a "custodial arrest." In these cases, the Court said, the police had the right to rely on their own judgment and initiative.

• In the 1974 case of *Michigan* v. *Tucker*, Justice Rehnquist argued for the majority that a statement made by a defendant who had not completely been advised of his rights could be used as evidence to locate a witness for the prosecution. Rehnquist believed that the procedures outlined in *Miranda* were safeguards of constitutional rights and not constitutional rights in themselves. Evidence that might help the prosecution's case, he concluded, could therefore be used without violating the rights of the defendant.

• The 1975 case of *Oregon* v. *Haas* involved a defendant

who had been given the proper *Miranda* warnings, but was told that he would not be able to talk to his lawyer until he reached the police station. In spite of the warnings, however, the suspect made statements about the crime on the way to police headquarters, and these statements were used against him in his trial. The Burger Court approved of the use of the statements and did not find that the *Miranda* restrictions had been violated.

• In a 1976 majority opinion, written by Justice Rehnquist, the Court declared that a private citizen publicly demeaned by the police as an "active shoplifter" had no recourse to federal courts to protect his reputation. The defendant's complaint, Justice Rehnquist pointed out, was nothing more than a "classical claim for defamation actionable in the courts of virtually every state." The defendant, he concluded, would do better to turn to the state courts for redress, rather than "invoke the procedural protection of the due process clause" of the Constitution.

• In another 1976 decision, reminiscent of earlier opinions written by Justice Harlan, Rehnquist stressed the importance of allowing the states to develop their own systems of criminal law. "Federal courts," he wrote, "must be constantly mindful of the 'special delicacy of the adjustments to be preserved between federal equitable power and state administration of its own law.' " A proper regard for federalism, he believed, required that the Supreme Court be reluctant to impose its will on the states, thereby destroying initiatives the states had taken on their own in criminal law.

In these decisions and others, the Burger Court was attempting to make law enforcement more efficient by reducing the restrictions placed on police work by the Warren

Court. It was also trying to lessen the Court's authority in the area of criminal procedure by turning some of that authority over to the states.

In none of its decisions, however, has the Burger Court overruled the *Miranda* requirements and made them obsolete. *Miranda* still stands as precedent, although many critics of the Burger Court, as we shall see, believe that it has been gutted of any real meaning or significance.

A Crescendo of Dissent

The remaining liberal justices issued strong dissents to the Burger Court's decisions on criminal law. Black, Brennan, Marshall, and Douglas joined in protesting the *Harris* opinion, which allowed statements made by a defendant before he was cautioned of his rights to be admitted in his trial and used to impeach his character. The *Harris* ruling, the dissenters believed, "goes far toward undoing much of the progress" the Court has made "in conforming police methods to the Constitution."

In the case where the Court denied help to a defendant who had been labeled by police as a shoplifter, Marshall and Brennan, dissenting, argued that the Court had committed a "regrettable abdication" of its responsibilities and "a saddening denigration of our majestic Bill of Rights." The Court, they said, should have heard the case and granted the defendant relief.

As a result of the Court's decision, they warned, police officers, "acting in their official capacities as law enforcers, could condemn innocent individuals as criminals and thereby brand them with one of the most stigmatizing and debilitating labels in our society."

In case after case, the liberals reiterated familiar themes.

Douglas accused the moderate and conservative majority on the Burger Court of "judicial activism" and "restructuring American law" for the purely "political reason" of carrying on a "war against crime." Marshall and Brennan believed that the Burger Court was in the business of creating a society "in which innocent citizens may be stopped, searched, and arrested at the whim of police officers who have only the slightest suspicion of improper conduct."

Justice Brennan was especially worried. He feared that the Burger Court had virtually emptied *Miranda* of principle and had rejected "*Miranda*'s basic premise that the techniques of police questioning and the nature of custodial surroundings produce an inherently coercive situation." The result, he said, could only be that police would now be able to violate the constitutional rights of defendants with impunity.

Brennan also believed that the Burger Court was in the process of allowing the "slow strangulation" of a defendant's rights under the exclusionary rule. Evidence that had once been inadmissible in court because it was illegally obtained, he pointed out, could now be used in trials. And this, he concluded, gave police carte blanche to obtain evidence in any manner they chose.

Many liberal editorialists and political commentators agreed with Brennan and the other dissenters. The Burger Court, they said, had done much to undermine the achievements of the Warren Court. But in a *New York Times* interview on April 9, 1976, the chief justice defended his Court and its record.

There has been "no significant change," the Chief Justice maintained, "in the Court's attitude toward the rights of criminal defendants in either four years or eight years or twelve years." The justices who have dissented, Burger added, "sometimes overstate the case" and give a false picture of the achievements of the Court in recent years.

Four months later, on August 11, Justice Lewis Powell likewise defended the Burger Court in an interview in the *New York Times*. What characterized the Court under Chief Justice Burger, Powell said, was a "leveling off" of judicial activism owing to the changes that had been made in the Court's membership since Warren's retirement.

"In recent years," Powell acknowledged, "the Court had decided a number of criminal cases differently from what might have been expected during the decade of the sixties." But it would be misleading and "alarmist," he claimed, to suggest that the Burger Court was responsible for "any significant weakening of the basic rights of persons accused of crime."

What has happened, Powell went on, is that the Burger Court has begun the evolution of a "more traditional" and "sounder" balance between "the rights of accused persons and the right of a civilized society to have a criminal justice system that is effective as well as fair."

The Burger Court Defends Criminals' Rights

In his *New York Times* interview, Chief Justice Burger pointed out that his Court had acted, in several instances, to extend the rights enjoyed by the accused. But these decisions, he believed, were not well known to the public or given wide currency in the press. For a fair understanding of the Burger Court, he implied, these too should be taken into consideration.

The chief justice mentioned no specific cases, but one he had in mind may have been a 1972 decision on prisoners seeking parole. In that decision, the Court declared that a hearing was required before a parolee could have his parole revoked. If no hearing was held, then the parolee's constitutional rights had been violated and he could seek redress for his grievances through the courts.

Another case the chief justice could point to in which the Burger Court had extended criminal rights was *Argersinger* v. *Hamlin,* also handed down in 1972. The right at issue in the *Argersinger* case was a defendant's "right to counsel," and the question before the Court was whether that right should apply to all criminal cases, serious or petty. Nine years earlier, in the *Gideon* decision, the Warren Court had applied the "right to counsel" only to cases of a serious nature.

Justice William Douglas delivered the *Argersinger* opinion for a unanimous Court. The *Gideon* case, Douglas pointed out, "involved felonies." But the reasoning behind the *Gideon* decision, he went on, "has relevance to any criminal trial, where an accused is deprived of liberty" and suggests "that there are certain fundamental rights applicable to all such criminal prosecutions."

The Court has decided, Douglas continued, that a lawyer is necessary even in "a petty offense prosecution" to ensure a fair trial. "Under the rule we announce today," he concluded, "every judge will know when the trial of a misdemeanor starts that no imprisonment may be possible, even though local law permits it, unless the accused is represented by counsel."

The *Argersinger* decision therefore extended the right to a lawyer to misdemeanors and petty cases. To those who might criticize the opinion for adding to the work load of attorneys and courts, the chief justice wrote a separate concurring opinion. "The dynamics" of the legal profession, Burger said, have "a way of rising to the burden placed on it." The defendant's right to counsel, he implied, outweighs any consideration of the increased work load that might fall on lawyers and courts.

The Death Penalty

In 1972 the Supreme Court handed down decisions in three related cases: *Furman* v. *Georgia, Jackson* v. *Georgia,* and *Branch* v. *Texas.* By a 5-to-4 vote in these cases the Court declared that the death penalty violated a person's rights under the Eighth Amendment, which states that "cruel and unusual punishment" shall not be inflicted upon citizens of the United States.

The five justices in the majority were holdovers from the Warren Court: Douglas, Marshall, Brennan, Stewart, and White. The four dissenters were the Nixon appointees: Burger, Blackmun, Powell, and Rehnquist. The decision can therefore be regarded as the last gasp of the Warren era. It should be pointed out, however, that the Burger Court has continued to work within the dictates of the decision and to knock down death penalty laws wherever it believes they amount to cruel and unusual punishment.

Each justice in the majority wrote a separate opinion outlining his views. According to Douglas, the death penalty was cruel and unusual because it depended on the "whim" of a jury. Justice Marshall, however, declared that the death penalty was unacceptable because it was "excessive" and morally questionable.

Justice Brennan wrote that the death penalty was "uniquely degrading to human dignity." And there was no reason to believe, he added, that it "serves any penal purpose more effectively than the less severe punishment of imprisonment."

Justice Stewart argued that "death sentences are cruel and unusual in the same way that being struck by lightning is cruel and unusual." There were many convictions for rape and murder in 1967 and 1968, he pointed out, yet only a few of these convictions resulted in the execution of the criminal. For a few to be executed while others are permitted to live for committing the same crime, he concluded, was a "wanton" and "freakish" application of law.

Justice White found that "the imposition and execution of the death penalty are obviously cruel in the dictionary sense." At one time, he declared, the death penalty was regarded as justified because of the social ends it served. But today, he went on, that is no longer the case. The imposition of the death penalty now amounted to no more than a "pointless" and "needless" extinction of life "with only marginal contributions to any discernible social or public purposes."

In his dissent, which summed up the views of the other dissenters, the chief justice argued that the Court should not consider the question of whether the Constitution forbids the death penalty. That should be up to the states. "If legislatures," he wrote, "come to doubt the efficacy of capital punishment, they can abolish it, either completely or on a selective basis."

Then, if new evidence "persuades them that they have acted unwisely, they can reverse their field and reinstate the penalty to the extent it is thought warranted." But an opinion handed down by the Court, he warned, offers no "flexibility" for change and imposes the same law on all the states.

The Court's decision left two paths open for the states to follow in rewriting their death-penalty statutes. One was to make the death penalty mandatory for certain crimes. This would eliminate the "wanton" and "freakish" aspects of the statutes that allowed some criminals to be executed and others to live.

The second path was to establish a two-stage process for all trials involving crimes punishable by death. During the first stage, the guilt or innocence of the defendant would be established. In the second, those found guilty would have sentence imposed. Of the thirty-five states that rewrote their death-penalty laws following the *Furman* decision, ten chose to establish mandatory rules, and the other twenty-five chose the two-stage process.

Four years after *Furman*, the two types of state laws came before the Supreme Court for consideration. In a 5-to-4 decision, the Court struck down mandatory laws from North Carolina and Louisiana. The laws from the two states had made death the required punishment for all first-degree murder cases.

Mandatory death penalties, the majority concluded, "simply papered over the problem of unguided and unchecked jury discretion." They did not ensure the criminal of his constitutional right to a fair trial. Mandatory laws were also undesirable because they gave "no significance to relevant facets of the character and record of the individual offender or the circumstances of the particular offense."

"In fixing the ultimate punishment of death," the majority concluded, room must be made for the consideration of "compassionate or mitigating factors stemming from the frailties of humankind." Consideration of the record of the defendant and the circumstances of the offense, the Court added, are a "constitutionally indispensable part of the process of inflicting the penalty of death."

On the same day it invalidated the mandatory death penalty, however, the Court declared the two-stage process constitutional. The cases came from Florida, Texas, and Georgia and were upheld by a vote of 7 to 2. Justice Stewart wrote the opinion for the majority.

The two-stage process, Stewart claimed, answered the problems that had been raised against the death penalty in the *Furman* decision. Under the two-stage process, he explained, the death penalty is no longer handed down "capriciously" or "arbitrarily." He continued:

> The new . . . sentencing procedures . . . focus the jury's attention on the particularized nature of the crime and the particularized characteristics of the individual defendant. While the jury is permitted to consider any aggravating or mitigating circumstances, it must find and identify at least one statutory aggravating factor before it may impose a penalty of death. . . . No longer can a jury wantonly and freakishly impose the death sentence; it is always circumscribed by the legislative guides.

Since the two-stage system allowed for the consideration of mitigating circumstances, Stewart concluded, it did not violate the injunction against cruel and unusual punishment.

Stewart made it clear that the Court did not oppose the death penalty in all cases. The death penalty, he wrote, "is an extreme sanction, suitable to the most extreme of crimes," such as murder, and would not be overruled by the high court. He then turned to the question of state criminal law, raised by the chief justice in his dissent in the Furman case. "Considerations of federalism," he wrote, "as well as respect for the ability of a legislature to evaluate" what the people of that state want and need make it wrong for the Court to overturn the death penalty. The states themselves must have the authority to make that decision.

Justices Brennan and Marshall, the Court's two remaining liberals, dissented from Stewart's opinion. According to

Brennan, American society had progressed to the point "where we should declare that the punishment of death, like punishments on the rack, the screw and the wheel, is no longer morally tolerable in our civilized society." Marshall added that he found the death penalty cruel and unusual punishment under any circumstances and therefore unconstitutional under the Eighth Amendment.

Since the Court handed down its decision on the two-stage process for imposing the death penalty, it has consistently followed the pattern outlined in that decision. In 1977 it struck down a Louisiana law that made the death penalty mandatory for anyone convicted of the first-degree murder of a policeman. In the same year it held that a Georgia law requiring the death penalty for the rape of an adult woman was excessive and therefore unconstitutional. And in 1978 the Court declared Ohio's death-penalty statutes for murder unconstitutional because the Ohio law did not allow for the consideration of mitigating factors.

CHAPTER TEN

Reapportionment and Race Relations

"Judicial restraint" has only limited applicability when the treatment of minorities, the fundamental liberties of individuals, or the health of the political process [is] at issue.
. . . Once fundamental rights have been recognized, there has never been a general reversal of direction by the Court, a going back against the trend of history—Former Associate Justice Arthur Goldberg in 1971.

In the last chapter, we saw how the Burger Court qualified but did not overrule the Warren Court's controversial decisions concerning criminal procedure. In Justice Powell's words, the new court wanted to establish a balance between the rights of the accused and society's need for an efficient criminal-justice system, not overturn Warren precedents. That the Burger Court was not going to reverse the Warren heritage was made clear in 1977 when the Court rejected a plea from twenty-two states to revoke the *Miranda* decision and its rulings. *Miranda*, the Court declared, would stand.

But what of the other two central features of the Warren revolution—reapportionment and desegregation? How did they fare in the hands of the Burger Court? Here too the new court qualified and modified Warren precedents but did not overturn them. In some instances, the Burger Court

145

added concepts and notions of its own to law that helped further the aims established by the Warren Court.

The hopes of many conservatives that the Warren years would be wiped out root and branch therefore were not realized. There was no doubt that the Burger Court was more conservative than the Warren Court. But its conservatism was not merely political; it was also judicial. And the chief tenet of judicial conservatism is to work *within* traditions handed down from earlier courts and not overturn them, however "liberal" those traditions might seem.

Reapportionment

An important decision involving reapportionment was handed down by the Burger Court in 1973 in the case of *Mahan* v. *Howell*. The case concerned Virginia's new reapportionment statute, established after the 1970 census on the basis of the Warren Court's rulings. The Virginia statute allowed as much as 16.4 percent deviation from the equal-population standard in the districts from which members of the legislature were elected.

Lower federal courts had rejected the Virginia plan and had argued that the 16.4 percent deviation was too large to be acceptable within the framework of "one person, one vote" established for legislative districts by the 1964 case of *Reynolds* v. *Sims*. The Burger Court, however, accepted the Virginia statute by a vote of 5 to 3. Justice Rehnquist wrote the opinion for the majority.

Justice Rehnquist pointed out that *Reynolds* v. *Sims* permitted some deviation between the populations of state legislative districts as long as those deviations were based on a *rational* state policy. Did the Virginia plan amount to a rational policy? Rehnquist believed that it did.

The Virginia plan for reapportionment was rational, he explained, because it respected the traditional political subdivisions of the state. The disparities in the voting districts resulted from reasonable efforts on the part of the state to allow for the accidents of history, geography, and other factors. No evidence, he added, showed that the state was trying to discriminate against some voters and favor others in the creation of the voting districts.

Moreover, Rehnquist went on, the large number of seats in the state legislature ensured that there would be "adequate statewide representation" for the various interests and groups that made up the state. For that reason, it was unnecessary to apply the test of "absolute equality" to legislative seats in Virginia. To apply the test of "absolute equality" to state voting districts, he warned, might impair "the normal functioning of state and local governments," and the Supreme Court should not be in the business of making government more difficult to operate than it already is.

Rehnquist concluded that the Virginia plan was acceptable to the Court and would be allowed to stand. He added, however, that the 16.4 percent disparity the Court was accepting in this instance might "well approach tolerable limits" and that higher disparities could prove unacceptable. He likewise emphasized that the Court's decision involved only state legislative districts and that far stricter standards were still required in the reapportionment of congressional voting districts.

Three liberal justices—Douglas, Marshall, and Brennan—dissented from Rehnquist's opinion. Equality of voting districts, they argued, was a constitutional mandate that could not be qualified or watered down. It was not reasonable, they concluded, for the Court to allow wide disparities between voting districts. Such disparities, they pointed out, always result in overrepresentation for some voters and underrepresentation for others.

Nor did the three liberals agree with Rehnquist's contention that traditional subdivisions of the state offered acceptable ways to form voting districts. Subdivisions like counties, they agreed, presented guidelines that could be used to initiate reapportionment, but traditional county lines had to be sacrificed in the name of equality of voting districts.

Later in the same year, 1973, the Burger Court firmly rejected the appeal from the liberal justices for greater standards of equality. In a majority opinion written by Byron White, the Court declared that reapportionment plans for state legislatures need not place an "unrealistic emphasis on raw population figures." Emphasis on population alone, White warned, would submerge other factors that "in day-to-day operation are important to an acceptable representation and apportionment arrangement."

The factors White had in mind were the historic and geographic subdivisions of the state, which he believed, for the sake of tradition, should not be ignored. A state, he added, must be allowed to operate within the political framework handed down from the past, if that framework is within limits deemed tolerable by the Court.

The standards set by the Supreme Court, White concluded, must remain flexible. Strict equality standards could only frustrate attempts to achieve the goal of fair and effective representation "by making the standards of reapportionment so difficult to satisfy that the reapportionment task is recurringly removed from legislative hands and performed by the federal courts."

When the Supreme Court entered the "hazards of the

political thicket," he went on, it did not intend that the federal judiciary would become bogged down "in a vast, intractable apportionment slough." But this is what might happen if the Court attempted to apply severe standards of equality to legislative reapportionment cases, he maintained.

White then asked the Court to look upon the problem of reapportionment with common sense. Common sense, he said, tells us that no one can say with confidence that "essentially minor deviations from perfect census population . . . will deprive any person of fair and effective representation in his state legislature." The Court, he implied, should move away from absolute standards and accept more practical solutions to the problem before it.

Had the Burger Court retreated from the Warren precedent in reapportionment? Not really. The strict equality standards for congressional districts still stood. What had happened in the case of state legislative districts was that the Burger Court had stepped into an opening offered by the Warren Court—which had declared that standards for reapportionment could be less strict in legislative districts—and used that opening to establish what it believed to be more practicable and realistic standards. The Warren precedent still stood, and the reapportionment decisions that Chief Justice Warren thought were the most significant work of his Court were still having their effect on the political life of the nation and the states.

Desegregation

The first desegregation case the Court heard under Chief Justice Burger was *Alexander* v. *Holmes Board of Education*. The case came from Mississippi, where thirty-three school districts requested an indefinite delay in the order to desegregate public schools. The school districts argued that they needed a transition period in order to ensure a safe and orderly changeover to integrated schools.

The *Alexander* case was significant because, for the first time in the history of desegregation cases, the federal government was arguing that the delay be granted. In 1968 Richard Nixon had won the presidency in large part because of support he received from southern voters. Now he wanted to establish a solidly Republican South, and one way to do that, he believed, was to show the southern states that his administration favored a go-slow approach on desegregation.

Nixon's Department of Health, Education and Welfare and Justice Department filed statements with lower federal courts in support of the delay. Without a delay, these statements warned, the Mississippi schools would face chaos, confusion, and "catastrophic educational setback." The lower federal courts granted the delay, provided the school districts took "significant steps during the next school year to put an end to segregation."

The case then came before the Supreme Court. Observers watched the Court closely. Chief Justice Burger was known to have a good record on civil rights, but he was also Nixon's first appointee to the Court. Would the new chief justice reflect the President's campaign to slow down the pace of desegregation? Or would the Court remain unanimous on desegregation decisions, as it had during the Warren era? Even if Burger stood alone in dissent on *Alexander,* it would show that Nixon had an opening on the court that might later widen until the Warren Court's desegregation precedents were overturned.

The decision that the Court handed down on October

29, 1969, was unanimous. The brief statement declared that the delay was not granted. In addition, it stated that "continued operation of the segregated schools under a standard of allowing deliberate speed for desegregation is no longer permissable." The phrase "deliberate speed," the Court believed, had allowed for too many postponements in the desegregation process. When it was adopted in 1955 in the *Brown* II case, the phrase meant that a "good faith" effort to desegregate schools should take place at a rate that preserved peace and order. But that had been almost fifteen years before, more than enough time for Mississippi officials to take steps toward desegregation if they were acting in good faith.

The *Alexander* decision ordered the thirty-three school districts to begin the operation of desegregated schools immediately. The aim of the desegregation process, the Court explained, was the creation of what it called "unitary school systems." Unitary school systems, the statement concluded were "systems within which no person is to be effectively excluded from any school because of race or color."

The next significant desegregation decision by the Burger Court, *Swann* v. *Charlotte-Mecklenburg County Board of Education,* was likewise unanimous. The case involved questions unanswered by the Warren Court. What remedies were permissable to end segregation? Should the busing of students to other schools be allowed? Should school districts be rearranged? What ratio of black and white students should a school have before it satisfied the desegregation requirement?

The *Swann* case came from North Carolina. The school system in question included the city of Charlotte and the surrounding rural area. In 1969 the entire system had 84,000 students—60,000 whites and 24,000 blacks—for a ratio of

71 percent to 29 percent. About 29,000 students were bused to school.

The problem was the distribution of the district's black population: about 21,000 of the 24,000 black students lived in the city of Charlotte. The other 3,000 lived in the rural areas of the county. The city's schools therefore were heavily black, and the rural schools were predominantly white. Three out of every four white students in the district attended "white" schools. Two out of every three black students attended schools that were 98 to 100 percent black.

In 1970 Judge James McMillan of the federal district court ordered the school district to bus an additional 13,000 students to attain more thoroughly desegregated schools. The additional students, he believed, would ensure that no school remained completely black and that the schools of the district would reflect the 71-to-29 ratio that was characteristic of the student population as a whole.

When the case came before the Court of Appeals for the Fourth Circuit, however, Judge McMillan's plan was delayed and then modified. The appeals court found that the busing of an additional 9,000 elementary school students imposed an unreasonable burden on the school board. The NAACP then appealed this decision to the Supreme Court, asking that the whole of McMillan's plan be reinstated.

Chief Justice Burger wrote the decision for the unanimous Court. The federal courts, Burger pointed out, became involved in desegregation plans only when school boards failed to live up to their obligation to end dual school systems that separated blacks from whites. In this case, it was clear that the school board had failed to act.

Judge McMillan, Burger went on, was only carrying out his responsibility as a federal judge when he developed his plan for the desegregation of the Charlotte and Mecklenburg County schools. His plan had been submitted after the school board had failed three times to come up with plans to end the present system. The Supreme Court, he concluded, accepts the district court's program for desegregation and orders it carried out.

Burger then turned to the alternatives a federal judge can choose from in developing a plan for the desegregation of public schools. These alternatives include school busing, establishing racial balances, and redistricting.

• *Busing.* The busing of students, Burger wrote, has been an "integral part of the public education system for years." It is therefore a remedy the Court would allow. However, he added, the Court recognizes that there are valid objections to busing. One is age. Clearly, the excessive busing of very young children is undesirable. Other objections are the "time" and the "distance of travel" that might be "so great as to either risk the health of the children or significantly impinge on the educational process."

• *Establishing Racial Balances.* Judge McMillan, Burger declared, had correctly used a racial balance of 71 to 29 as "a starting point in the process of shaping a remedy" to segregation in the Charlotte-Mecklenburg County school district. Racial balances, however, are not a matter of constitutional principle. "The constitutional command to desegregate schools," the chief justice explained, "does not mean that every school in every community must always reflect the racial composition of the school system as a whole."

• *Redistricting.* Burger said that the Court approved of gerrymandering school districts as an alternative open to school boards to achieve desegregation. School districts could be rezoned to provide a greater mixture of white and black students.

The Court acknowledged, he continued, that schools attended by students of only one race were not always the result of official segregation policies. Some neighborhoods were black, others white. Nevertheless, he maintained, every effort must be made "to achieve the greatest possible degree of actual desegregation and . . . the elimination of one-race schools."

Burger recognized that these remedies might prove "administratively awkward, inconvenient and even bizarre in some situations and may impose burdens on some." But, he added, "all awkwardness and inconvenience cannot be avoided in the interim period when the remedial adjustments are being made to eliminate the dual school system." The transition to desegregated schools will not be easy, he concluded.

Most of Burger's comments in the *Swann* decision stood firmly within the Warren Court's precedents on desegregation. But the chief justice also sounded a new note. Throughout the decision, he emphasized that the remedies he suggested were interim corrective measures to bring an end to the vestiges of segregation. The remedies, he implied, need not become a permanent part of school board policy.

What, then, if resegregation gradually took place after the old dual system had been dismantled? "Neither school authorities nor district courts," Burger concluded, "are constitutionally required to make year-by-year adjustments of the racial composition of student bodies once the affirmative duty to desegregate has been accomplished and racial discrimination through official action is eliminated from the system."

This does not mean, he added, "that federal courts are

without power to deal with future problems." What it does mean, however, is that "in the absence of a showing that either the school authorities or some other agency of the state has deliberately attempted to fix or alter demographic patterns to affect the racial composition of the schools," then further action by the district court should not be necessary.

The *Swann* decision was handed down in 1971. In 1972 and again in 1974 the Court reiterated the doctrine begun by *Swann*. The 1972 decision declared that "judicial power ends when a dual system has ceased to exist." The 1974 opinion stated that federal district courts had "fully performed" their function of providing "the appropriate remedy for previous racially discriminatory attendance patterns" once they had established a "racially neutral pattern" in school systems.

The new doctrine outlined in *Swann* and developed in the two later cases was the Burger Court's attempt to draw a line that limited the Court's jurisdiction in desegregation matters. A more limited jurisdiction was necessary, the Court believed, to keep the federal judiciary from becoming bogged down in desegregation cases. It was likewise needed to allow more flexibility to local school boards and authorities.

But the new policy struck the liberals who remained on the Court as a retreat from the standards set by the Warren Court. In their dissents to these cases, Justices Marshall and Brennan argued that the Court's responsibility required more than overseeing the establishment of "racially neutral patterns" or the end of the "dual system of education." The Court's duty, they believed, was to implement lasting desegregation programs that prevented a return to segregated schools, and this could not be done without a constant judicial review of desegregation policies throughout the country.

What worried the liberals above all was that the new policy signaled the beginning of a willingness on the part of the Burger Court to withdraw the Court's commitment to the desegregation of all aspects of American life. Would the new majority of conservative and moderate justices abandon the Court's drive for equality? Would they slow down the movement for the establishment of civil rights to such a degree that the movement no longer had any meaning?

These fears have not been justified. In case after case, the Burger Court has tended to stand within the Warren tradition concerning race relations and the civil rights of black Americans. The Burger Court has not subtracted from those rights and in several instances has added to them. The Burger Court's approach to the extension of these rights, however, has been more cautious and circumspect and contains less of the sweeping moral idealism that characterized the Warren Court.

Among other problems, the Burger Court has addressed discrimination in employment, the segregation of private schools, de facto segregation, and the continuing controversy that its own decision on school busing aroused.

• *Employment discrimination.* In a 1971 case upholding the 1964 Civil Rights Act, the Burger Court declared that a company's requirement of a high school diploma or a general intelligence test for employment discriminated against black employees. These barriers to employment, the Court said, were "artificial, arbitrary, and unnecessary" and therefore unconstitutional.

Four years later, in 1975, the Court said that back pay

was a proper remedy for black workers who had been held back from advancement or increased wages because of racial discrimination. It likewise allowed seniority rights to persons denied advancement because of race.

• *Segregation in Private Schools.* In 1973 the Burger Court declared that the state of Mississippi's policy of giving free textbooks to private schools that practiced segregation was unconstitutional. Such action, the Court maintained, was equivalent to state support for segregation and therefore unacceptable. The next year it forbade the city of Montgomery, Alabama, to allow its public parks to be used by private schools practicing racial segregation.

Then, in 1976, the Court found that private schools practicing discrimination violated the 1866 Civil Rights Act, which gave "all persons within the jurisdiction of the United States the same right . . . to make and enforce contracts . . . as is enjoyed by white citizens." The 1866 law clearly means, the Court said, that all citizens, black or white, have the right to enter into contractual agreements, and these agreements include the right to enter a private school.

• *De Facto Segregation.* The Warren Court's drive had been against segregation that was upheld and enforced by law, or *de jure* segregation. The Burger Court declared that in some cases de facto segregation, which existed "in fact" but not under law, was unconstitutional. When school boards could be shown by *purpose* or *intent* to have developed policies that led to segregated schools, then that segregation was illegal.

• *School busing.* The Court's endorsement of school busing as a remedy for segregation aroused widespread protest in the 1970s. Parents' groups and others argued that busing is unreasonable and undesirable because it removes children from neighborhood schools and often requires them to travel long periods of time each day to and from their assigned schools.

The Burger Court did not back down from its commitment to busing as a remedy to segregation. But in new cases involving busing, it declared that a remedy for segregation should not exceed the extent of the violation. It therefore turned down busing plans it considered too drastic and stated that busing should be used only in school districts where discrimination was clearly practiced and had resulted from action taken by school boards. When one district was found to practice discrimination, it was not to be merged with another district where discrimination was not practiced. "Only if there has been a systemwide impact" by discrimination in the public schools, Justice Rehnquist explained in a 1977 opinion, "may there be a systemwide remedy."

The Bakke Case: Reverse Discrimination

One problem raised by the drive for racial equality is "reverse discrimination." Are white citizens discriminated against when special efforts—called "affirmative action"— are made to raise the status of racial minorities? Are the rights of white citizens violated when they are excluded from an educational program they are qualified to enter because a number of positions in the program have been reserved for minority group members?

In 1978 the Court turned to this dilemma. The complaint came from California. On two occasions, Allan Bakke, a white, was denied admission to the medical school at the University of California at Davis. The Davis medical school had openings for one hundred students; sixteen of the openings were set aside for "economically and educationally disadvantaged minority applicants."

At thirty-eight, Bakke was older than the other applicants and already had a degree in engineering. He was highly qualified and had scored higher on the school's entrance requirement than any of the minority applicants who had been accepted for admission. Those requirements covered a variety of factors including undergraduate grades, scores on the Medical College Admissions Test, community involvement, and character.

Believing that his rights had been violated when he was denied admission, Bakke filed suit. The California Supreme Court heard his case and ordered him admitted to the school. The case then went to the federal court system and the Supreme Court.

The *Bakke* case was decided by a closely divided vote, 4–1–4. Justice Powell cast the swing vote in a two-part decision. Four justices—Burger, Stevens, Stewart, and Rehnquist—joined by Powell, said that Bakke's rights had been violated and ordered him admitted to the school. But four other justices—Brennan, Blackmun, Marshall, and White—were joined by Powell in endorsing affirmative action programs.

Both sides had won in the case; neither had lost. Bakke received the right to enter medical school, which he did. At the same time, affirmative action programs were upheld and given the approval of the high court.

The four justices who voted to grant Bakke admission argued that Bakke's rights under the Civil Rights Act of 1964 had been violated. Justice Stevens wrote the opinion expressing their views. The university, Stevens pointed out, had excluded Bakke from admission on the basis of race. At the same time, the university acknowledged that it received federal financial assistance. The terms of the Civil Rights Act of 1964, he concluded, are crystal clear: "Race cannot be the basis of excluding anyone from participation in a federally funded program."

In joining their opinion, Justice Powell added comments of his own on the constitutionality of "racial quotas" in admissions policies. "Explicit racial classification," Powell noted, is not always unconstitutional. "But when a state's distribution of benefits or imposition of burdens hinges on . . . the color of a person's skin or ancestry, that individual is entitled to a demonstration that the challenged classification is necessary to promote substantial state interest."

In the case of the medical school's classification system, Powell wrote, he could find no substantial state interest that had been promoted. The desire to remedy wrongs done by past discrimination, he said, was not sufficient, because it was based on "an amorphous concept of injury that may be ageless in its reach into the past." Moreover, there was no means to determine which injured minority groups should receive "heightened judicial solicitude" and which should not.

Powell thus regarded the Davis admissions plan as unconstitutional, but his belief that some racial quota programs could be constitutional led him to join the four justices who supported affirmative action. When was a program of explicit racial classification constitutional, he asked? And answered: when it contained the element of *flexibility.*

Where flexibility was absent, as in the *Bakke* case, the university's admissions policy imposed disadvantages on individuals like Bakke, "who bear no responsibility for whatever harm the beneficiaries of the special admissions program are thought to have suffered." An affirmative action policy, Powell concluded, must be flexible enough to bend so that the rights of no individual are harmed.

Powell carefully limited affirmative action programs to cases of proven discrimination. The four justices he joined in supporting affirmative action, however, were more liberal in regard to what they believed to be the needs of minority groups. Unlike Powell, they believed that the university's desire to remedy the past wrongs of discrimination was justification enough for the establishment of a policy favorable to blacks and other minority groups.

"In order to get beyond racism," Justice Blackmun explained, "we must first take account of race. . . . And in order to treat some persons equally, we must treat them differently." A school's admissions policy, he believed, should be left up to the school itself and should not be a subject for the Court to issue a judgment on. "The administration and management of educational institutions," he concluded, "are beyond the competence of judges and are within the special competence of educators."

Justice Brennan believed that "race conscious" programs could be instituted, even where there had been no specific violation of the Constitution. "Government," he wrote, "may take race into account when it acts not to demean or insult any racial group, but to remedy disadvantages cast on minorities by past racial prejudice, at least when appropriate findings have been made by judicial, legislative, or administrative bodies with competence to act in this area."

What the *Bakke* decision revealed about the Burger Court was its moderation and its judicial modesty. In the decision, the Court moved slowly to make progress toward solving a very complex problem—the balance that must be struck between the rights of whites and the rights of minorities.

Perhaps the key word in the opinions written by the justices was "competence." Justice Blackmun questioned the competence of the Court to deal with educational matters. Justice Powell questioned its competence to deal with "the kind of variable sociological and political analysis" necessary to establish just programs of affirmative action. Without proper competence, they implied, the Court should be reluctant to step into issues that have no clear-cut answers.

CHAPTER ELEVEN
Four Important Cases

Six months ago if you had asked me what the Supreme Court should and should not do, I probably could have given you a quick answer. But now, I am not so sure. New problems arise that the authors of the Constitution did not anticipate. But the answers to the problems ought to be made to fit an existing pattern; a new pattern should not be made. The hardest question is when the Court should step in—Statement by Chief Justice Warren Burger, not long after he joined the Court.

The Constitution gives the President the right to appoint members of the Supreme Court, and Presidents have used this privilege to establish the kind of Court they believe the nation needs. Frequently, however, Presidents find that the individuals they appoint do not turn out to be the kind of justices they had hoped for. There seems to be no certain way of predicting the judicial philosophy a nominee will take once he or she is seated on the high court. When asked about his appointment of Chief Justice Earl Warren, whom he had regarded as a conservative Republican, President Eisenhower responded that "it was the biggest damn fool mistake I ever made."

Former President Nixon may have similar sentiments about Chief Justice Burger and the three other justices he appointed to the Court. The Burger Court refused to grant the Nixon administration the right to restrain publication of top-secret documents whose publication the government argued might damage the security of the United States. It likewise struck down several aspects of Nixon's "war on crime," a "war" the President believed was important to the domestic stability of the nation.

And it was the Burger Court that overturned restrictive abortion laws—a move Nixon had long opposed—and handed down a decision in the Watergate affair that led directly to the resignation of President Nixon under threat of impeachment. In its own way, the Burger Court proved to be an activist Court in the Warren tradition, carefully protecting its right to judicial review and to say what the Constitution is.

The Case of the Pentagon Papers

The Sunday edition of the *New York Times* for June 13, 1971, carried the headline: "VIETNAM ARCHIVE: PENTAGON STUDY TRACES 3 DECADES OF GROWING U.S. INVOLVEMENT." Inside the newspaper were six pages of government communiqués, presidential orders, position papers from the state and defense departments, and other information regarded as highly secret by the federal government.

The data published by the *Times* was part of a study ordered by former Secretary of Defense Robert McNamara and covered the administrations of Presidents Truman, Eisenhower, Kennedy, and Johnson. The next day, June 14, the *Times* carried more of the information and promised to publish everything that came into its hands. Altogether, there were forty-seven volumes of data, a total of 2.5 million words. The message it carried was explosive, and revealed repeated mismanagement of the Vietnam War and deception by officials at the highest levels of government.

The *Times* decided to publish the material only after it had determined that none of the "secrets" it contained might damage or harm the current war effort in Vietnam. Since all the material concerned past administrations, the *Times* deemed it publishable. But in Washington, the Nixon administration looked on with alarm. Nixon was concerned about the leak that had turned the information over to the press. If the press could obtain this classified information, he wondered, were other government secrets about the war likewise in danger of publication?

On Monday, June 14, the day the *Times* published the second installment of "the Pentagon Papers," as the material was dubbed by the press, Attorney General John Mitchell called the *Times* and asked that the newspaper print no more. If the *Times* continued to publish the material, he warned, its editors would risk being convicted under the espionage law, which carried a fine of $10,000 and ten years' imprisonment. There was no doubt, he added, that the government would prosecute, because publication of the Pentagon Papers was causing "irreparable injury to the defense interests of the United States."

The next day, however, the *Times* published the third installment of the papers and included an account of the threat it had received from the attorney general. The same day, the government took the case to federal district court in Manhattan and asked for an injunction against the editors of the newspaper. The district judge issued a temporary restraining order on the *Times* and set a hearing on the case for Friday, three days away.

Obeying the court order, the *Times* stopped publication

of the Pentagon Papers. But on Friday, the *Washington Post* began to publish its own account of the secret material, followed a few days later by the *Boston Globe.* The Associated Press sent the *Washington Post* accounts to its offices around the world.

The Justice Department took the *Post* to federal district court in Washington to stop publication. But the Washington judge refused to issue a temporary restraining order, as the New York judge had done. Such an order, he claimed, would "impose a prior restraint on publication of essentially historical data" and violate freedom of the press.

The Justice Department then took the case to the Appeals Court in Washington, which voted 2 to 1 to impose restraint on publication. Meanwhile, the New York judge refused to issue a permanent injunction against the *Times,* but allowed the temporary injunction to be extended until higher courts considered the case. With both the *Post* and the *Times* under restraint of publication, the case came before the Supreme Court.

The cases, *New York Times* v. *United States* and *United States* v. *The Washington Post,* came before the Court on June 24. Six days later, on June 30, the Court delivered its opinion. Six justices voted in favor of the newspapers; three voted against. It was the opinion of the majority that the government had failed to meet "the heavy burden of showing justification" for restraint of publication of the Pentagon Papers.

Each of the nine justices wrote separate comments, outlining his views on the cases. It was the opinion of Justices Black and Douglas that freedom of the press was absolute and could not be abridged by the government in any circumstances. "Every moment's continuance of the injunctions against these newspapers," Black wrote, "amounts to a flagrant, indefensible, and continuing violation of the First Amendment."

Justices Brennan, Stewart, and White thought that clear and immediate emergencies provided circumstances in which the government could restrain the press, but added that the Pentagon Papers did not represent such a case. The test for prior restraint, Stewart contended, was that publication of the material would result in "direct, immediate, and irreparable damage to our Nation or its people."

Justice Marshall pointed out that Congress had twice refused to give a President authority to prohibit publication of material disclosing matters of national security or to make such disclosures criminal. The Court, Marshall concluded, should not carry out actions that Congress has specifically refused to carry out.

The chief complaint of the three justices who voted against the papers—Burger, Blackmun, and Harlan—concerned the haste with which the decision was handed down. Chief Justice Burger believed that the press did not enjoy an absolute freedom from prior restraint and warned that the Pentagon Papers might contain something dangerous to national security that could have been "flushed out had they been properly considered in the trial courts, free from unwarranted deadlines and frenetic pressures."

Justice Harlan believed that the cases should have been returned to lower federal courts for consideration. Justice Blackmun argued that "What is needed here is a weighing, upon properly developed standards, of the broad right of the press to print and of the very narrow right of the government to prevent." The Court, he implied, had not had sufficient time to carry out this "weighing" of the evidence.

In an interview after the decision was handed down, the chief justice declared that the Court had been "actually unanimous" and that the differences that separated the justices were minor. Given more time to consider the Pentagon Papers, he implied, all the justices might have joined an opinion preventing the government from restraining the publication of the material.

Electronic Surveillance and Privacy

In the Omnibus Crime Control and Safe Streets Act of 1968, Congress granted statutory authority to law officers for the use of wiretaps and electronic surveillance. But Congress likewise ordered that every wiretap that police intended to install had to have the approval of a federal judge, who would issue a warrant granting permission.

In 1972 a case involving a violation of this law came before the Supreme Court for consideration. Known as *United States* v. *U.S. District Court, Eastern Michigan,* it concerned three leftist radicals who had been charged with conspiracy to destroy government property. The three radicals sued for disclosure of the evidence against them that had been collected, they believed, by illegal wiretapping.

The government admitted that no warrants had been issued approving the wiretaps that had taken place. But the wiretaps had been authorized by the attorney general of the United States as part of an investigation of subversive domestic organizations. They were an essential element in the administration's program to maintain the security and stability of the American government against groups that wanted to overthrow it.

The wiretaps were therefore a reasonable exercise of presidential authority, the government argued, and were permissible in circumstances where the security of the nation was threatened. In extreme emergencies, the government concluded, prior judicial approval for wiretapping should not be necessary and might damage the ability of law officials to gather information secretly and efficiently.

Two lower federal courts rejected the government's claim, and the case came before the Supreme Court. In an 8-to-0 decision the high court likewise turned down the government's plea. Justice Rehnquist abstained from an opinion because as an assistant attorney general in the Nixon administration, he had participated in the government's anti-subversive program. Justice Powell wrote the opinion for the Court.

Powell noted that among Americans there was a "deep-seated uneasiness and apprehension" that electronic surveillance techniques like wiretapping would be used "to intrude upon cherished privacy of law-abiding citizens." This uneasiness, Powell continued, led him to believe that government officials responsible for the investigation and prosecution of crime should not be the sole judges of when "constitutionally sensitive" acts, like wiretapping, should be used.

Government officials, he warned, "may yield too readily to pressure to obtain incriminating evidence and overlook potential invasion of privacy and protected speech," which are guaranteed by a "convergence" of First and Fourth Amendment rights. It was the responsibility of the Court to defend citizens from overzealous law officers who would overlook constitutional rights in their vigorous pursuit of evidence.

Moreover, Powell went on, electronic surveillance runs the risk of violating constitutional rights no matter what its purpose might be. This infringement of rights takes place, he believed, whether the surveillance is part of a criminal investigation or part of an "on-going intelligence gathering"

mission. In either instance, the government may have acted
to undermine basic and fundamental rights.

Powell believed that electronic surveillance violated the
right to speak in dissent of government policies. History
has abundantly shown, he pointed out, that governments
tend "to view with suspicion those who most fervently dis-
pute its policies." It has also shown, he added, that governments will resort to various methods to help silence or
destroy dissent.

In this case, the government had defended its illegal
wiretaps on the basis of a need to protect the "national
security." Powell found this defense "vague" and unacceptable. Private dissent, he maintained, "no less than public
discourse is essential to our free society." It should not be
sacrificed in the name of an amorphous concept like "national security."

The Supreme Court, he concluded, believes that lawful
private dissent is protected by the Constitution. Those who
dissent lawfully should not be subjected to the "dread" of
"an unchecked surveillance power." Nor should "the fear of
unauthorized official eavesdropping" be allowed to "deter
vigorous citizen dissent and discussion of Government action in private conversation."

The decision by the Court did not forbid wiretapping in
all instances. It merely upheld the requirement that wiretaps had to be approved by a federal judge. Nevertheless
the decision directly challenged Nixon's assertion of an absolute right to violate established law in what he regarded
as a period of national crisis. It declared that the President's
law-and-order campaign had to follow established procedure in order to keep within the rights guaranteed by the
Constitution.

The Abortion Cases

On January 22, 1973, the Burger Court handed down a decision on an issue never before considered by the Supreme Court: abortion. The cases, *Roe* v. *Wade* and *Doe* v. *Bolton*, came from Texas and Georgia where restrictive abortion laws prevented women from having abortions except under extreme conditions. "Roe" and "Doe" were fictitious names, used to protect the identities of the women challenging the restrictive laws.

The Court struck down the Texas and Georgia laws by a vote of 7 to 2. Justice Harry Blackmun wrote the decision for the majority. "The Constitution," he wrote, "does not explicitly mention any right of privacy." Nevertheless, he went on, "in a line of decisions . . . the Court has recognized that a right of personal privacy, or a guarantee of certain areas or zones of privacy, does exist under the Constitution."

It was clear, Blackmun claimed, that only those personal rights that could be called "fundamental" or "implicit in the concept of ordered liberty" could be included under the guarantee of personal privacy. What were the areas that the Court believed warranted a right to privacy? They were activities relating to marriage, procreation, family relationships, and child-rearing and education.

Blackmun found the right to privacy implicit in several parts of the Constitution—in the First, Fourth, and Ninth Amendments and elsewhere. But it was in the Fourteenth Amendment's concept of personal liberty that he found freedom "broad enough to encompass a woman's decision whether or not to terminate her pregnancy."

The section of the Fourteenth Amendment Blackmun referred to stated:

No State shall make or enforce any law which shall abridge the privileges or immunities of citizens of the United States; nor shall any State deprive any person of life, liberty, or property, without due process of law; nor deny to any person within its jurisdiction the equal protection of the laws.

Blackmun concluded that a woman had a right to terminate her pregnancy if she so chose and that the state should not interfere with that right. He added, however, that the right to an abortion is not an absolute right. There are times, he said, when the state "may properly assert important interests" in preventing abortions.

Blackmun declared that during the first trimester of pregnancy (the first three months), government had no interest sufficient to warrant interference in a woman's decision to abort. In the second trimester, however, when medical statistics showed that a mother was more likely to be harmed physically by an abortion, then government had the authority and compelling interest to protect her health. In the second trimester, therefore, the state could step in and pass laws regulating the practice of abortion.

In the third trimester, the period that medical science determined the fetus could live on its own outside the body, the state's compelling interest became the protection of the life of the fetus. In order to protect the fetus during the last three months of pregnancy, Blackmun concluded that the states could pass laws forbidding abortion, except in instances where abortion was necessary to protect the life or health of the mother.

Blackmun regarded the decision as based on the Constitution and a careful reading of the best medical literature on abortion. Critics, however, believed otherwise. They denounced the Court's ruling as a venture in "lawmaking" comparable to the most controversial decisions of the Warren Court. The Court had not interpreted the Constitution, they claimed, for abortion is nowhere mentioned in the Constitution. Rather the majority of the justices had written their own opinions into the law of the land.

The abortion decision had intruded into one of the most sensitive areas of human concerns: moral and religious values. For the opponents of abortion, abortion is quite simply murder. "How many millions of children," asked Terence Cardinal Cooke of New York City, "prior to their birth will never live to see the light of day because of the shocking action of the majority of the United States Supreme Court?" And Cardinal Krol of Philadelphia added: "It is hard to think of any decision in the two hundred years of our history which has had more disastrous implications for our stability as a civilized society."

United States v. Nixon

The year 1974 saw a head-on clash between the President and the Supreme Court. The occasion was the Watergate affair. The special prosecutor in the case, Leon Jaworski, was at an impasse. To complete his investigation of the Watergate scandal, Jaworski needed tapes of private White House conversations between President Nixon and his chief aides. Only then, he believed, would he know for certain if the President and his assistants had violated law.

The problem was that the President refused to relinquish the tapes. In April 1974 Jaworski obtained a subpoena from Federal District Court Judge John Sirica, ordering Nixon "to surrender them to the prosecutor." The President declined, arguing executive privilege. The chief executive, he explained, must be allowed to conduct the affairs of state in private, out of the public eye. To turn over the tapes would damage the functioning of his administration.

Judge Sirica set 4:00 P.M. Friday, May 24, as the deadline for the President to appeal for a ruling by the Court of Appeals of the District of Columbia, the customary next step in the judicial process. But Jaworski, impatient for a decision in the case, made the extraordinary move of asking the Supreme Court for a judgment. Permission to "leapfrog" a lower court is permissible in cases of "imperative public importance," but is rarely granted.

But Jaworski pleaded an imperative need for the tapes. Some of Nixon's aides were up for trial, he explained, and it would be impossible for them to have a fair trial unless the evidence in the recordings was available. He likewise pointed out that his requests were for *specific* tapes, memoranda, and other materials. He was not on a "fishing expedition" for any or all of the tapes in the President's possession.

The Supreme Court voted to hear the case before it passed through the appeals court. On June 8 the justices heard oral arguments. The lawyers for the President, led by James St. Clair, a prominent attorney from Boston, reiterated the President's claims to executive privilege. The separation-of-powers doctrine, they said, meant that the private material of the executive branch of government should not be viewed by officials of another branch. Jaworski reiterated his need for the material to carry out his responsibilities as special prosecutor.

On July 24 the Court handed down its decision. It was unanimous, 8 to 0, with Justice Rehnquist abstaining because of his former association with the Nixon administration. The chief justice delivered the opinion. The Court rejected Nixon's claims to absolute executive privilege and ordered the material turned over to Jaworski. It was the first time in American history that a writ of the Court ran against the President. Before then, it was assumed that the chief executive was immune to the legal process.

Chief Justice Burger looked back to the first great decision of the Marshall Court. Like Chief Justice Marshall in 1803, Burger declared, "We . . . affirm that it is 'emphatically the province and duty' of this Court 'to say what the law is' " with regard to the issues raised by this case. The Court, he said, has the authority to consider the matter of executive privilege.

Burger acknowledged that the President's right to executive privilege did exist. "A President and those who assist him," he explained, "must be free to explore alternatives in the process of shaping policies and making decisions and to do so in a way many would be unwilling to express except privately." Burger likewise believed that executive privilege was "fundamental to the operation of government and inextricably rooted in the separation of powers under the Constitution."

The right of executive privilege therefore does exist, Burger continued, but it is a limited right and cannot be held as absolute in all circumstances. "Neither the doctrine of separation of powers," he went on, "nor the need for confidentiality of high level communications, without more, can sustain an absolute, unqualified presidential privilege of immunity from judicial process under all circumstances."

In this case, the chief justice pointed out, executive privilege had not been used to protect military, diplomatic, or other "sensitive national security secrets." It had been used to protect material related to a criminal prosecution, and this, Burger explained, was the problem. The right of executive privilege was not broad enough to grant the President power to impair "the fair administration of criminal justice."

Nixon's concept of executive privilege, Burger went on, would allow too much power to flow to the presidency, thereby upsetting "the constitutional balance of a workable government." The executive would be strengthened at the expense of the judiciary. This, he believed, should not be allowed to happen. The President's "generalized assertion of privilege must yield to the demonstrated, specific need for evidence in a pending criminal trial.

"Without access to specific facts," Burger wrote, "a criminal prosecution may be totally frustrated." If the judiciary is to carry out its responsibility, it must have the right to obtain evidence pertinent to a given case. And this right to evidence, he concluded, outweighs the President's claim of executive privilege.

Burger ordered the President to submit to Judge Sirica's subpoena and turn the tapes over to the special prosecutor. The unanimous decision of the Court was significant because it allowed the President no room to ignore the order. A minority opinion in his favor might have encouraged Nixon to ignore the majority decision.

The President submitted to the Court ruling and relinquished the tapes. The information they contained was explosive and led to his resignation from the presidency seventeen days later. At the time, four members of the court were Nixon appointees. Three of them voted against the President's claims of executive privilege. One abstained.

CHAPTER TWELVE

The Character of the Burger Court

The nature of our system, which seems to have escaped notice occasionally, must make manifest to judges that we are neither gods nor godlike, but judicial officers with narrow and limited authority. Our entire system of government would suffer incalculable mischief should judges attempt to oppose the judicial will above that of the Congress and the President, even were we so bold as to assume we can make better decisions on such issues—Chief Justice Warren Burger.

On Saturday, July 3, 1980, the *Washington Post* carried an article by Supreme Court observer Fred Barbash under the headline, THE BURGER COURT STILL LACKS A THEME. The only theme that could be discovered behind the decisions of the Burger Court, Barbash claimed, "was the lack of a theme." A decision that could be regarded as a victory for conservatives was followed by a victory for liberals. There was no discernible philosophy guiding the Court's work. The result, he concluded, was confusion. Lower courts were left without sufficient guidelines to interpret law, and few major issues were resolved decisively.

One year later, Barbash was of a different mind. His July 3, 1981, article on the Court was headlined, BURGER COURT MAY BE ONTO TRUE MISSION. What was the "mission" that Barbash believed the Burger Court had found during its

177

1980–81 term? It was, he wrote, "a firm commitment to a drastically curtailed role for the federal judiciary as a check on the rest of the government." The new Burger Court, he added, "is a deferential court that 'knows its place' in the scheme of government, not a court that tries to carve a place" for itself. "It is a humble court, finally a Burger Court, not an Earl Warren Court."

Barbash pointed to three 1981 cases in which the Court had shown itself to be "humble" and "deferential."

• *The Case of Philip Agee.* Agee is a former CIA agent who is now an outspoken critic of the agency. He is associated with publications dedicated to the exposure of CIA activity and of undercover agents. The state department revoked Agee's passport, regarding him as a danger and menace to American interests. The question before the Supreme Court was whether or not the state department had the power to revoke Agee's passport.

In his majority opinion in the case, Chief Justice Burger denied the Court's jurisdiction in the affair. "Matters intimately related to foreign policy and national security," he wrote, "are rarely proper subjects for judicial intervention. . . . Matters relating 'to the conduct of foreign relations are so exclusively entrusted to the political branches of government as to be largely immune from judicial inquiry or interference.' "

• *A Case of Overcrowded Prisons.* In a decision involving the placing of two prisoners in cells designed for one, Justice Powell declared, "Courts certainly have a responsibility to scrutinize claims of cruel and unusual confinement. . . . However, courts cannot assume that state legislatures and prison officials are insensitive to the requirements of the Constitution."

• *Women and the Draft.* In a case concerning the question

of whether Congress can exclude women from the draft, Justice Rehnquist wrote, "The Congress is a co-equal branch of government whose members take the same oath we do to uphold the Constitution of the United States." Rehnquist believed that Congress had the authority to exempt women from the draft and that it was not the duty of the Supreme Court to "correct" this view.

In the first case, the Court bowed before the authority of the state department, in the second before that of the state legislatures, and in the third before that of Congress. Clearly, Barbash wrote, the Burger Court was on a track different from the one followed by the Warren Court.

The Character of the Burger Court

Barbash was correct in his analysis of the Burger Court's character but inconsistent when he described its origin. In the first part of his 1981 article, he implied that the Court discovered its true mission after the 1980 landslide victory of Ronald Reagan. The Court had read the election returns, Barbash wrote, and realized it had a mandate for conservatism.

In another part of his article, however, Barbash claimed that the 1980–81 change in the Burger Court had begun in 1973 after the enormous public backlash to the abortion decision. The Court had been so stung by that response, he suggested, that it had begun to take a more prudent and cautious approach to the law.

Barbash is on firmer ground when he traces the character of the Burger Court back to 1973. By that time a new majority of justices had come into being, formed by two moderate holdovers from the Warren Court, Stewart and White, and the four Nixon appointees. The new majority was uncertain, because the moderates from the Warren years sometimes joined the liberals. Nevertheless, in case after case, the Burger Court now toned down and qualified Warren Court precedents in criminal law, reapportionment, and race relations. The character of the Burger Court had begun to emerge, but its development was slow and gradual.

What are the characteristics of the Burger Court? In the first place, it is a Court that has attempted to return to the tradition of "judicial restraint." Its philosophy recalls the views expressed by Justice John Harlan in his vigorous dissents to many Warren Court decisions. In his dissent in the reapportionment case of *Reynolds* v. *Sims,* Harlan had accused the Warren Court of having a "mistaken view of the Constitution and the constitutional function of this Court." He continued, "This view, in a nutshell, is that every major social ill in this country can find its cure in some constitutional 'principle' and that this Court should 'take the lead' in promoting reform when other branches of government fail to act. The Constitution," Harlan had concluded, "is not a panacea for every blot upon the public welfare," and the Supreme Court should not be regarded "as a haven for reform movements."

It is this view that characterizes the judicial restraint of the Burger Court. Coupled with this view is an equally important element in the philosophy of judicial restraint— the belief that the Court's "competence" extends only so far and that, when that limit of competence is reached, the Court must defer to other authorities. In the words of Chief Justice Burger, which opened this chapter, judges must realize that they are "neither gods nor godlike, but judicial officers with narrow and limited authority."

Another characteristic of the Burger Court is its respect

for federalism. Here again, the present court is following the lead of Justice Harlan. Harlan once accused the Warren Court of cutting "deeply into the fabric of our federalism," thereby destroying the delicate relationship between the states and the federal government that was established by the Constitution.

The Burger Court has taken steps to restore this "delicate relationship" by deferring to state governments and allowing state legislatures more room to innovate and experiment with law. The Burger Court believes that a decentralization of power is in order, a flow of power away from the federal judiciary and back to the states.

Thus a key characteristic of the Burger Court is its attempt to restore what it believes to be proper balance in government: proper balance between the federal judiciary and the other branches of the federal government and proper balance between the federal judiciary and the power of the states.

A final characteristic of the Burger Court's judicial restraint is the high regard the Court has shown for *stare decisis*. This regard has led the Burger Court to work within precedents handed down from the Warren years, even when it disagreed with them. Thus Justice Harlan refused to overturn the *Miranda* decision, even though he dissented against it when it was handed down in 1966. *Miranda*, he believed, had become established practice, not to be overturned on a whim or the passions of the moment.

Respect for *stare decisis* also led Chief Justice Burger and Justices Powell and Rehnquist to accept strict requirements for the reapportionment of congressional districts even though they believed the precedent to which they adhered was wrong. If they had been on the Court when the precedent was handed down, they said, they would

have voted against it. But for the sake of stability and continuity in the process of law, they would now support it.

The judicial modesty of the Burger court and its caution
and prudence have led advocates of judicial activism to
charge the Court with mediocrity and spinelessness. The
Burger Court, the critics say, is "leaderless and unpredict-
able," a "maybe" Court afflicted with the inability to say
what the law is with courage and conviction.

To prove their charges, the critics point out that plurality
decisions, or rulings that command no majority of justices,
have increased enormously under Chief Justice Burger. By
the end of its 1979–80 term the Burger Court had handed
down eighty-eight plurality decisions. In the previous 180
years the Court had handed down eighty-seven. Thus in an
eleven-year period the Burger Court broke the record established in the whole history of the Supreme Court.

Responding to these criticisms, Justice Lewis Powell in
1980 asked the critics of the Burger Court just what kind of
Court they wanted. "If . . . one's liberty were at stake,"
Powell asked, would one like "to be judged by a Court
whose members were dominated by a willful chief justice?"
Moreover, he continued, "what confidence could a litigant
have in a Court that decided cases according to some consistently applied philosophy or 'theme' rather than the facts
of his case and the applicable law."

Powell believed that the numerous plurality decisions of
the Burger Court should not be regarded as proof of inde-
cisiveness and uncertainty. Rather, they reflected that the
Court had become a "marketplace of ideas" where all aspects of an issue were aired and discussed. This aspect of
the Burger Court, he concluded, was a strength, not a
weakness. It showed that the Court appreciated the com-

plexity of the problems it considered and was not tempted to look for simple, fixed solutions.

The Present and the Future of the Court

In the summer of 1981 Justice Potter Stewart announced his resignation from the Court. He had been appointed justice in 1958 by President Eisenhower and had proved to be a moderate in judicial philosophy, a liberal in support of *Miranda* and the other criminal procedure cases, and a conservative in his dissents on the cases involving school prayer and Bible reading.

To replace Stewart, President Reagan appointed Sandra Day O'Connor, a federal appeals court judge from Arizona. She became the 102nd justice to serve on the Court, and the first woman. A moderately conservative Republican, Justice O'Connor nevertheless was an outspoken supporter of equal rights for women and, as a member of the Arizona state legislature, had voted for liberal abortion legislation.

President Reagan is likely to have the opportunity to appoint more new members to the high court. At present, five justices are over seventy—Burger, Brennan, Blackmun, Powell, and Marshall—and the average age at which past justices have retired from office or died while on the Court is seventy. The President is likely to choose individuals who share his conservative views. If he does, the complexion of the Court will be determined for some time to come.

At this time there are at least twenty bills before Congress designed to trim judicial authority. Their sponsors hope to strip the Court of its power to deal with issues like legalized abortion, state-sponsored prayer, and court-ordered busing. These bills would counteract the most controversial decisions of the Warren and Burger Courts. They would make the philosophy of judicial activism almost impossible to carry out and write judicial restraint into the law of the land.

The threat of such legislation may cause the Burger Court to move more rapidly in the direction it has already moved, toward conservatism and judicial restraint. Just as the Warren Court helped appease liberal sentiment in its drive for equality and fairness under law, so the Burger Court may find its responsibility to be in the appeasement of the conservative drive for the restoration of traditional patterns of lawmaking.

Suggested Further Reading

The Congressional Quarterly's *Guide to the United States Supreme Court** (Washington 1980) is an excellent resource on all aspects of the high court. Another helpful guide, though limited to the Warren Court, is Charles Sheldon's *The Supreme Court: Politicians in Robes** (Beverly Hills: Glencoe Press, 1970). A useful general history of the Court is provided by Barbara Habenstreit in her *Changing America and the Supreme Court** (New York: Julian Messner, 1974).

The doctrine of judicial restraint is defended by Raoul Berger in his *Government by Judiciary* (Cambridge, Mass.: Harvard University Press, 1977) and by Louis Lusky in *By What Right?* (Charlottesville, Va.: Michie, 1975). A favorable view of Warren Court activism is found in A. T. Mason, *The Supreme Court from Taft to Burger* (Baton Rouge: Louisiana State University Press, 1979).

A superb study of *Brown* v. *Board of Education* is Richard Kluger's *Simple Justice** (New York: Knopf, 1975). The role of the Court in American life is also the subject of other important books, three of which are Richard Funston, *Judicial Crises: The Supreme Court in a Changing America* (Cambridge, Mass.: Schenkman, 1974); Leonard Levy, editor, *Judicial Review and the Supreme Court* (New York: Harper & Row, 1967); and Robert G. McCloskey, *The Modern Supreme Court* (Cambridge, Mass.: Harvard University Press, 1972).

Archibald Cox, *The Warren Court* (Cambridge, Mass.: Harvard University Press, 1968) is excellent on the Court led by the

*An asterix (*) denotes books of special interest to young readers.

most controversial chief justice of modern times. On the same subject see Philip Kurland, *Politics, the Constitution, and the Warren Court* (Chicago: University of Chicago Press, 1970).

Unfortunately, there is no general study on the Burger Court comparable to the studies of the Warren Court, but for a book on one aspect of the changes that have taken place since the Warren years see Leonard Levy, *Against the Law: The Nixon Court and Criminal Justice* (New York: Harper & Row, 1974).

Very interesting and illuminating are the memoirs written by and about Supreme Court justices. Among these are Earl Warren, *The Memoirs of the Chief Justice Earl Warren** (New York: Doubleday, 1977); Hugo Black, *My Father, a Remembrance** (New York: Random House, 1975); and William O. Douglas, *The Court Years, 1939–1975** (New York: Random House, 1980).

Index

Abortion, Burger Court on, 171–73, 179, 183

Activism vs. restraint, 20–23, 45–46, 68–69, 101–3, 129, 137, 182, 184

Agee, Philip, 178

Agnew, Spiro, 117, 118

Alexander v. Holmes Board of Education, 149–51

American Civil Liberties Union (ACLU), 29

Appointments, 14; to Burger Court, 121–24, 163–64, 179, 183; to Warren Court, 27–31, 50–51n, 67n, 84. *See also names of justices*

Argersinger v. Hamlin, 139

Armstrong, Scott, 120–21

Avant Garde (magazine), 118–19

Baker v. Carr, 61–63, 67 and *n*

Bakke case, 158–61

Bayh, Birch, 114

Becker, Frank, 96

Bible reading in public schools, Warren Court on, 85, 90–97

Black, Hugo, 28–29, 31, 56, 61, 64, 75, 88–89, 122, 136, 166

Black justices. *See* Marshall, Thurgood

Blackmun, Harry, 116, 121, 123, 140, 161, 162, 167, 171–72, 183

Branch v. Texas, 140

Brandeis, Louis D., 23

Brennan, William, 51n, 57, 62, 123, 136, 137, 140, 143, 144, 147, 155, 161, 183

Brethren, The (Armstrong, Woodward), 120 and *n*, 121

Brown II, 42–43, 151

Brown v. Board of Education, 27–57, 124n; background of, 31–35; decision enforcement in, 42–43, 48–57, and Fourteenth Amendment, 37–42, 47, 50,

55; and Little Rock, Ark., 48–51; reaction to, 44–57

Burger, Warren E., appointed Chief Justice, 84, 112–13, 121

Burger Court, 107–84; on abortion, 164, 171–73, 179, 183; on busing, 151–52, 153, 157–58; character of, 177–84; on civil rights, 145, 149–58; on criminal justice, 129–44, 145; on electronic surveillance and privacy, 168–70; justices of, 121–24, 163–64, 179, 183 (*see also names of justices*); on Pentagon Papers, 164–68; purpose of conservatism in, 146, 180–184; on reapportionment, 145, 146–49, 180, 181; on reverse discrimination, 158–61; on segregation, 145, 149–58; transition to, 109–24; Warren Court compared to, 9–11, 182; Warren Court criticized by, 130–36, 181; and Warren precedents, 132–36, 137, 145, 146, 149, 154, 180, 181, 182; on Watergate affair, 164, 173–176. *See also names of cases*

Burton, Harold, 30, 54n

Busing, Burger Court on, 151–52, 153, 157–58

Byrd, Robert, 85

Cahn, Edmond, 22

Carswell, G. Harold, 114–16, 117

Circuit courts, 36n, 113

Civil rights: *Alexander v. Holmes Board of Education*, 149–51; *Brown v. Board of Education*, 27–57; Burger Court on, 145, 149–58; *Green* case, 56–57; *Griffin* case, 56, 57; *Plessy v. Ferguson*, 32–33, 34, 41, 51 and *n*; *Swann* decision, 151–155; *Sweatt v. Painter*, 34–35;

Civil rights *(cont.)*
Warren Court on, 27–57, 100, 104; *Watson v. Memphis*, 52. *See also* Educational segregation; Segregation
Civil Rights Act (1875), 32, 33, 53–54
Civil Rights Act (1964), 52–54, 156, 159, 160
Civil Rights Movement, 52–53
Clark, Tom, 30, 54, 62, 73, 90–93, 123*n*
Colegrove, Kenneth, 60–61
Communism, 30, 98
Congress: and reapportionment, 58–70, 147; on religion in school, 96–97; responsibilities of, 20–21; Supreme Court limitations on, 13, 16–19, 22; Supreme Court limited by, 14, 15, 20–21, 23
Conservatism, purpose in Burger Court, 146, 180–84
Constitution, 10; Article III, 13–14; Supreme Court established in, 13–15; Supreme Court power over, 13, 14, 15–23, 45–46, 101–2. *See also amendments*
Cooper v. Aaron, 50–51
Corwin, E.S., 99
Counsel, right to. *See* Right to counsel
Court Years, The (Douglas), 121
Cox, Archibald, 25
Criminal justice: *Argersinger v. Hamlin*, 139; *Branch v. Texas*, 140; Burger Court on, 129–44, 145; *Escobedo v. Illinois*, 76–77, 80–81, 83, 84, 129, 132–133; *Furman v. Georgia*, 140, 142–43; *Gideon v. Wainwright*, 74–75, 76, 80, 82, 130, 139; *Harris v. New York*, 133–34, 136; *Jackson v. Georgia*, 140; *Mapp v. Ohio*, 72–73, 80; *Michigan v. Tucker*, 134; *Miranda v. Arizona*, 77–84, 129, 132–36, 137, 181; *Oregon v. Haas*, 134–35; Warren Court on, 71–84, 129, 130–36, 140
Criminal Justice Act (1964), 82

Davis, John W., 38–39
De facto segregation, 157
De Tocqueville, Alexis, 9, 10
Death penalty, 112, 117; Burger Court on, 140–44

"Declaration of Constitutional Principles," 47–48
Desegregation. *See* Segregation
Dirksen, Everett, 69, 96–97, 111, 112
Discrimination. *See* Civil rights; Employment discrimination; Reverse discrimination; Segregation
District courts, 36 and *n*, 49; and segregation, 152–55
Doe v. Bolton, 171
Douglas, William O., 29–30, 31, 61, 63, 107, 136, 137, 139, 140, 147; impeachment proceedings against, 117–21; resignation of, 123
Draft, and women, 178–79

Education and religion, Warren Court on, 85–98
Educational segregation: *Alexander v. Holmes Board of Education*, 149–51; *Brown v. Board of Education*, 27–57; and busing, 151–52, 153, 157–58; *Cooper v. Aaron*, 50–51; de facto, 157; *Green* case, 56–57; *Griffin* case, 56, 57; private school, 157; *Swann* decision, 151–55; *Sweatt v. Painter*, 34–35. *See also* Civil rights; Segregation
Eighth Amendment, Burger Court on, 140, 144
Eisenhower, Dwight, 28, 49, 164; Supreme Court appointments of, 50*n*, 54*n*, 163, 183
Electronic surveillance and privacy, Burger Court on, 168–70
Employment discrimination, Burger Court on, 156–57
Engel v. Vitale, 86–89, 96
Ervin, Sam, 96
Escobedo v. Illinois, 76–77, 80–81, 83, 84, 129, 132–33
Evidence, admissibility of: Burger Court on, 133–35; *Harris v. New York*, 133–34, 136; *Miranda v. Arizona*, 77–84, 129, 132–36, 137; *Oregon v. Haas*, 134–35; Warren Court on, 77–84, 129, 132–36. *See also* Criminal justice; Interrogation, criminal
Executive privilege, Burger Court on, 174–76

Federalist Papers, The, 14–15, 19
Fifteenth Amendment, 31, 32, 33, 56, 63 and *n*
First Amendment, Warren Court on, 85–88, 93, 97–98
Ford, Gerald: and impeachment proceedings against Douglas, 118–20; Supreme Court appointments of, 123
Fortas, Abe, 110–13, 114, 116, 117
Fourteenth Amendment, 31, 32, 33; and abortion, 171–72; and *Brown v. Board of Education*, 37–42, 47, 50, 55
Fourth Amendment: Burger Court on, 134; Warren Court on, 72–73
Frankfurter, Felix, 21, 29, 60–61, 66, 67 and *n*
Freedom of press, and Pentagon Papers, 164–68
Furman v. Georgia, 140, 142–43

Gideon v. Wainwright, 74–75, 76, 80, 82, 130, 139
Ginzburg, Ralph, 119
Goldberg, Arthur, 67, 76–77, 103–4, 110, 145
Goldwater, Barry, 119
Gordon, Rosalie, 45–46
Graham, Billy, 95–96
Gray v. Sanders, 63
Green case, 56–57
Griffin case, 56, 57

Hamilton, Alexander, 15–17, 19
Harland, John Marshall (grandfather), 32–33, 51*n*
Harlan, John Marshall (grandson), 50–51*n*, 67, 68, 80, 81–82, 101–3, 122, 167, 180, 181
Harris v. New York, 133–34, 136
Haynesworth, Clement, 113–14, 116, 117
Helms, Jesse, 97
Holmes, Oliver Wendell, 109
Hoover, Herbert, Supreme Court appointments of, 117
Housing, segregation in, 54–55
Hruska, Roman, 115
Hughes, Charles Evans, 13

Impeachment, 14, 109; proceedings against Douglas, 117–21
Interrogation, criminal, Warren Court on, 76, 77–80, 81–82, 84. *See also* Evidence, admissibility of

Jackson, Robert, 30, 50–51*n*, 60*n*
Jackson v. Georgia, 140
Jaworski, Leon, 173, 174, 175
Jay, John, 16
Jefferson, Thomas, 19–20, 68, 89*n*
Johnson, Lyndon, 53, 82, 164; Supreme Court appointments of, 109–12, 123*n*
Judicial activism vs. restraint, 20–23, 45–46, 68–69, 101–3, 129, 137, 182, 184
Judicial review, 15–20
Justices. *See* Appointments; *names of justices*

Kennedy, John, 82, 164; Supreme Court appointments of, 67*n*

Legislature. *See* Congress; Senate
Lewis, Albert, 95
Little Rock, Ark., and *Brown v. Board of Education* decision, 48–51

Maidson, James, 15–16, 89 and *n*, 90
Mahan v. Howell, 146
Mapp v. Ohio, 72–73, 80
Marbury v. Madison, 17–19
Marshall, John, 17–19, 20, 68, 100, 175
Marshall, Thurgood, 37–40, 45, 123–124*n*, 136, 137, 140, 143, 144, 147, 155, 167, 183
Mason, A.T., 33, 99, 100, 104–5
Michigan v. Tucker, 134
Minton, Sherman, 30–31, 51*n*
Miranda v. Arizona, 77–84, 129, 181; as precedent in Burger Court, 132–36, 137, 145
Mitchell, John, 120, 121, 165
Moral Majority, 97
Murphy, Frank, 22, 61
Murray v. Curlett, 90–91*n*

National Association for the Advancement of Colored People (NAACP), 29, 46, 114, 115, 152
New Deal, 30, 31
New Republic (magazine), 29
New York Times, 137, 138; and Pentagon Paper publication, 164–68
New York Times v. United States, 166–68

Newmyer, R. Kent, 14
Nineteenth Amendment, 63, 64n
Nixon, Richard, 84, 170; and Pentagon Papers, 165; resignation
of, 118, 164, 176; Supreme
Court appointments of, 84,
112–17, 121–23, 124, 130,
140, 150, 163–64, 179; and
Watergate affair, 164, 173–76

Obscenity, Warren Court on, 98
O'Connor, Sandra Day, 183
Omnibus Crime Control and Safe
Streets Act (1968), 83–84, 168
Oregon v. Haas, 134–35

Parole, Burger Court on, 138–39
Pentagon Papers, 164–68
Plessy v. Ferguson, 32–33, 34, 41, 51
and *n*
Points of Rebellion (Douglas), 119
Pornography, 119; Warren Court on,
98
Powell, Lewis, 122, 123, 138, 140,
145, 159, 160, 162, 169, 170,
178, 181, 182, 183
Prayer in public schools, Warren
court on, 85–90, 93–97
Precedent, 54, 129; and judicial activism, 22–23; and judicial restraint, 20–21; *Miranda* case
as, 132–36, 137, 145; Warren,
Burger Court interpretation
of, 132–36, 137, 145, 146,
149, 154, 156, 180, 181, 182
President: Supreme Court appointments by, 14; Supreme Court
limitations on, 13, 16–17, 19,
22; Supreme Court limited by,
14, 15. *See also names of presidents*
Prison overcrowding, 178
Pritchett, C. Hermann, 89n
Privacy. *See* Abortion; Electronic surveillance; Right to privacy
Private school segregation, Burger
Court on, 157
Public places, segregated, 32, 51–52,
53–54
Public school bible reading and
prayer, Warren Court on, 85–
98

Racial discrimination. *See* Civil rights;
Employment discrimination;
Segregation

Reagan, Ronald, 97, 179; Supreme
Court appointments of, 183
Reapportionment: *Baker v. Carr*, 58,
61–63, 67 and *n*; Burger
Court on, 145, 146–49, 180,
181; *Gray v. Sanders*, 63; *Mahan v. Howell*, 146; *Reynolds
v. Sims*, 64, 65, 146, 180; Warren Court on, 58–70, 145–46;
Wesberry v. Sanders, 64
Reed, Stanley, 29, 51n
Rehnquist, William, 122–23, 134,
135, 140, 146–48, 169, 174,
179, 181
Religion in school: *Engel v. Vitale*,
86–89, 96; *Murray v. Curlett*,
90–91n: *Schempp* decision,
90–93, 94; Warren Court on,
85–98
Restraint vs. activism, 20–23, 45–46,
68–69, 101–3, 129, 137, 182,
184
Reverse discrimination, and *Bakke*
case, 158–61
Reynolds v. Sims, 64, 65, 146, 180
Right to counsel: Burger Court on,
139–40; Warren Court on, 74–
75, 76, 80–81, 130, 133, 139
Right to privacy: Burger Court on,
134; Warren Court on, 72–73,
80
Right to remain silent, Warren Court
on, 75–77, 79, 133
Roe v. Wade, 171
Roosevelt, Franklin, Supreme Court
appointments of, 28–31, 122
Rosenberg, Julius and Ethel, 117

Schempp decision, 90–93, 94
*School District of Abington Township
v. Schempp*, 90–93, 94
Search and seizure: Burger Court on,
134; Warren Court on, 72–73
Segregation, 114, 122; *Alexander v.
Holmes Board of Education*,
149–51; *Brown v. Board of
Education*, 27–57; Burger
Court on, 145, 149–58; and
busing, 151–52, 153, 157–58;
constitutionality of, 37–43;
Cooper v. Aaron, 50–51; de
facto, 157; and decision enforcement, 42–43, 48–57,
150–58; *Green* case, 56–57;
Griffin case, 56, 57; in housing, 54–55; *Plessy v. Ferguson*, 32–33, 34, 41, 51 and *n*.;

private school, 157; *Swann* decision, 151–55; *Sweatt v. Painter*, 34–35; in travel and public places, 32, 51–52, 53–54; Warren Court on, 27–57, 150; *Watson v. Memphis*, 52. *See also* Civil rights; Educational segregation
Senate, Supreme Court appointments approved by, 14
Seventeenth Amendment, 63 and *n*, 64*n*
Sirica, John, 173, 174, 176
Sixth Amendment, and Warren Court, 74–75
"Southern Manifesto, The," 47–48
Spellman, Cardinal, 95, 96
Stare decisis, 20, 22, 181
State courts and criminal justice: Burger Court on, 130, 135, 141–44; Warren Court on, 71–72, 74, 80, 84
State redistricting. *See* Reapportionment
Steamer, Robert, 100
Stevens, John Paul, 123, 159
Stewart, Potter, 54 and *n*, 55, 93–94, 123, 140, 141, 143, 167, 183
Supreme Court, 36*n*; activism vs. restraint in, 20–23, 45–46, 68–69, 101–3, 129, 137, 182, 184; Burger and Warren compared, 9–11, 182; changes in, due to Warren Court, 99–105; constitutional power of, 13, 14, 15–23, 45–46, 101–2; establishment of, 13–15; and judicial review, 15–20; legislative branch limited by, 13, 16–19, 22; limits on, 14–15, 20–21, 23; power of, 10, 13–23; president limited by, 13, 16–17, 19, 22; presidential appointments to, 14 (*see also names of presidents*); Senate approval of appointments to, 14; transition, Warren-Burger, 109–24. *See also* Burger Court; *names of cases*; Warren Court
Swann v. Charlotte-Mecklenburg County Board of Eucation, 151–55
Sweatt v. Painter, 34–35

Talmadge, Herman, 48, 96
Thirteenth Amendment, 31, 32, 33, 55

Thornberry, Homer, 110
Transportation, segregated, 32, 51–52, 53–54
Truman, Harry, 35, 164; Supreme Court appointments to, 30–31

United States v. The Washington Post, 166–68
United States v. U.S. District Court, Eastern Michigan, 168–70

Vietnam War, 111; and Pentagon Papers, 164–68
Vinson, Frederick, 34
Voting districts. *See* Reapportionment

Warren, Earl, 25, 29*n*, 100; appointed Chief Justice, 25, 27, 28; resignation of, 84, 109–12
Warren Court, 25–105; Burger Court compared to, 9–11, 182; Burger criticism of, 130–36, 181; on civil rights, 27–57, 100, 104; on criminal justice, 71–84, 129, 130–36, 140; justices of, 27–31, 50–51*n*, 67*n*, 84 (*see also names of justices*); on obscenity and pornography, 98; as precedent for Burger Court, 132–36, 137, 145, 146, 149, 154, 156, 180, 181, 182; on reapportionment, 58–70, 145–46; on religion in school, 85–98; on segregation, 27–57, 150; Supreme Court change due to, 99–105; and transition to Burger Court, 109–24. *See also names of cases*
Washington Post, 177; and Pentagon Paper publication, 166–68
Watergate affair, Burger Court on, 164, 173–76
Watson v. Memphis, 52
Wesberry v. Sanders, 64
White, Byron, 67*n*, 81, 123, 140, 141, 148–49
Whittaker, Charles, 51*n*, 67*n*
Wiretapping, Burger Court on, 168–170. *See also* Watergate affair
Women, and draft, 178–79
Woodward, Bob, 120–21

ABOUT THE AUTHOR

Stephen Goode was born in Elkins, West Virginia. He holds a B.A. from Davison College, an M.A. from the University of Virginia, a Ph.D. from Rutgers University, and has studied in Vienna and Budapest. Mr. Goode was a lecturer in history at Rutgers University. For the last seven years he has lived in the Washington, D.C. area, where he pursues his interest in government and politics. He is the author of a number of books in these fields, including *Guerrilla Warfare and Terrorism, Assassination: Kennedy, King, Kennedy* and *The New Congress.*